Better Homes and Gardens®
501 DECORATING IDEAS UNDER $100

ISBN 978-0-470-59546-6

Printed in the United States of America

10 9 8 7 6 5 4 3 2 1

Note to the Readers:
Due to differing conditions, tools and the individual skills, John Wiley & Sons, Inc. assumes no responsibility for any damages, injuries suffered, or losses incurred as a result of following the information published in this book. Before beginning any project, review the instructions carefully, and if any doubts or questions remain, consult local experts or authorities. Because codes and regulations vary greatly, you always should check with authorities to ensure that your project complies with all applicable local codes and regulations. Always read and observe all of the safety precautions provided by manufacturers of any tools, equipment, or supplies, and follow all accepted safety procedures.

Better Homes and Gardens®

501 DECORATING IDEAS UNDER $100

WILEY

John Wiley & Sons, Inc.

Contents

.......................➤

on the cover
Give your rooms color and vintage charm using the quick and easy ideas starting on *page 108.*

organize

embellish

reimagine

1 hang time A colorful brooch brings a dramatic touch to this piece of artwork. Add a ribbon hanger to your frame, perhaps gluing a jewel at the top. Mount the ribbon to the wall using a removable adhesive strip. If the frame is heavy, mount it separately and then simply adhere the ribbon to the wall above.

hidden gems

Give your space a touch of star quality with dazzling artwork made from old jewelry.

2 photo finish Decorative pins and belt buckles make fun frames for family photos. Remove the buckle's center stile if needed, and tape a photo to the back. To prop your pieces, cut ½-inch strips of cardboard, fold into triangles, and then tape to the back.

3 spread your wings Butterfly brooches like these are too beautiful to keep tucked away in a jewelry box. Let them take flight as wall art by creating a pseudo-scientific display. Paint a gesso-finish artist's canvas with water-thinned dark umber paint and then rub it off. Use a graphite pencil to draw lines depicting the wingspans.

more ideas

Try these other fashion statements that flaunt costume-jewelry charm.

4 Wind bracelets or necklaces around napkins as unique napkin rings.

5 Dangle various baubles from a chandelier.

6 Showcase pretty pieces in a shadow box and hang as art.

7 Remove backs from earrings and glue to magnets or thumbtacks to post on magnetic or tack boards.

8 Trim a lampshade with a strand of pretty beads.

For more project details, see "Dig In" on page 56.

unlikely art

Conventional or not, anything you find visually inspiring deserves to be on display.

9 quick study A vintage atlas found at a yard sale provides great wallpaper for this bedroom. Souvenirs from school trips and other family adventures complement the walls. The adjoining bath applies the same technique, using magazine pictures instead of maps. Use a quality wall primer before you apply the maps and pictures with wallpaper paste—when you decide to redecorate, you'll find it much easier to remove them.

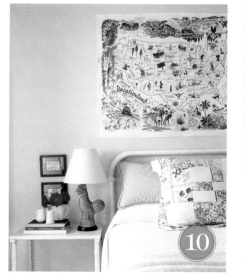

10 tablecloth tapestry
A midcentury tourist tablecloth fills the space over this bed and adds character to the room. Make coordinating pillows by cutting tablecloths into squares and piecing them together randomly. If you have small furnishings, such as chairs or ottomans, use old tablecloths to cover the cushions.

11 kid stuff Turn pages from a children's book into a wall display. Oversize French script on a white background makes this arrangement bold and graphic. (Use a photocopier to enlarge the text to the size you need.) Clear frames with clips keep the look clean and hold down the cost.

12 evolving art Surround a large piece of corkboard with framing material and change the artwork as often as you like. In this family dining area, postcards collected on vacations bring color to the wall and conversation to every meal.

13 simpler samplers Framed scraps of crewelwork are a fresh and easy approach to traditional samplers. Look for vintage embroideries at antiques shows or check out fabrics stores for upholstery and drapery textiles. You'll need only a small swatch to make a handsome showing.

14 round and round Crafted from urethane, these ready-made ceiling rosettes are lightweight and easy to hang. Displayed at eye level and painted in shades of yellow, the discs add style and a punch of color to this sitting room. Look for similar pieces at your local home center or online at sites like **wishihadthat.com**.

15 by the book When it comes to colorful artwork, take a page (or two) from your favorite book. Or showcase a book jacket by displaying it on a stand alongside other treasures. In a library-shelf lineup, only the spine gets recognition. But solo or as part of a grouping on easels, book jackets are sure eye-catchers.

16 giant gerbera If you love bold color and you're not afraid to use it, dress a small bath with a large hand-painted flower. Freehand-paint the design on the wall, or cut a pattern from paper and draw around it. Fill in the shapes with wall or acrylic crafts paint, alternating vivid shades of orange, red, yellow, and purple.

Dig through your closet and attic to find **everyday treasures** to display as art.

17 mirror images

Turn your old family photos into an intriguing wall display by showing them off in vintage silver and ceramic frames. Scan the original photos into your computer and use photo software to resize, crop, and change the color. Mount the prints onto plates, trays, and other pieces using glue or decoupage medium.

do-it-
yourself
decoration

When you're looking for
creative ideas for your walls,
think outside the frame and use
everyday items in clever ways.

21

18 behind the scenes When you see what's framing these pretty still-life china plates, you may be surprised to find ceiling medallions. Easy to find in a variety of sizes, these composite fixtures are designed to dress up the ceiling plates of chandeliers. We opted to mount dinner plates in the centers using E6000, a strong adhesive. To ensure that the glue creates a good bond, we marked off the area where the back of each plate would touch and painted only outside it.

20 vacation shadow box Protect your beach treasures in a shadow box and relive your vacation year-round. For the background, use a scrap of vintage wallpaper or ask your home center for discontinued wallpaper books with small sample pieces. Just adhere your sea fans, sea horses, and shells to the paper and assemble the box.

21 updated traditional Classic bird prints can be pricey once they're professionally matted and framed. We used pages from a book and mounted them in inexpensive clip-edge frames (backed with scrapbook paper when needed to get the right size). The $35 book had hundreds of images to choose from and plenty to share with friends.

19 budget-wise tapestry When a French textile or Belgian tapestry isn't in the budget, take a trip to a fabrics store. Look for texture and pattern in off-the-bolt yardage that resembles expensive weavings. Add a border around the edges, sew drapery rings to the top, and hang it from a bold rod.

22 rack up compliments

Typically used to display collectibles, these shelves now are the collection! Watch for small spice racks and shelves at resale shops and yard sales. Paint them in a variety of soft cottage colors and hang them en masse.

23 canned humor

Don't throw out cans once you've finished their contents. The shiny metal-and-ribbed pattern gives these wall-mounted vases a modern industrial look. Drill holes in the sides of the cans and join them together with bolts. Add a few holes in the top backs for hanging. As shown with flowers or over a desk for office supplies, contemporary can art can't be beat.

25 shutterbug Cottage style and old shutters are naturals together. Try hanging shutters horizontally for displaying photographs, postcards, letters, and clippings. If years of paint prevent your louvers from closing tightly enough to hold the papers, use a small piece of double-stick tape to keep items in place.

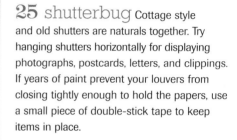

24 place-mat parade At only a dollar each, these place mats add a fun factor to the dining room out of proportion to their cost. Simply drill holes and connect the mats, column by column, with a ball-link chain between mats. Hang the connected columns from nails. This easy technique also works for room dividers and window treatments.

on the
MAP

Globes and maps are fun collectibles that appeal to travelers and homebodies alike. These projects give your home international appeal.

26 round the clock
Don't think a timeworn globe is useless. Make one hemisphere of a separated globe into a three-dimensional clock, using the hole where the stand once supported it as a fitting for the clock mechanism and hands.

27 picturesque backdrop

Remember the pull-down maps from grade school? If you're lucky enough to find one at a flea market, use it as wallpaper.

28 tourist traps Ceramic tiles

collected at favorite vacation spots make a colorful addition to an outdoor table. They're perfect for resting glasses of iced tea.

29 pull out the stops Turn

a small chest of drawers into an oasis for all things travel-related. Switch ordinary drawer pulls for knobs resembling small globes.

32 map it out Perk up a pair of

small plain metal buckets with maps glued to their sides. Out-of-date maps are prime candidates for this project, and the small pails are the ideal size to hold flatware and napkins on a buffet table.

30 continental divide See

the world from the comfort of home with inexpensive maps that double as window coverings. Hold the maps in place with archival double-stick tape or glazier's points.

31 get framed Vintage maps

make nice framed artwork. Look for one in good condition and place it underneath heavy books to flatten it. Then spray-mount the map to an archival backing before framing it.

For more project details, see "Dig In" on page 56.

type casting

Originally designed for printing, vintage letterpress blocks can raise your home decor's character. Express yourself with these projects.

33 name game Personalize a jewelry box with a name or monogram by gluing small letterpress blocks directly to the top of the lid using an adhesive designed for both wood and metal. As a bonus, the blocks serve as a handle for lifting the lid.

34 hot stuff Turn letterpress blocks into a trivet or coaster. Lay out various blocks to create a pattern you like and then simply glue them together.

35 run the table Send a message to partygoers with a wordy centerpiece. Spell out a greeting with blocks, varying their heights for interest. Glue the pieces together or leave them loose for more flexibility.

36 stuck in the middle

Create a one-of-a-kind side table by sandwiching wooden blocks between a pedestal table and a piece of glass cut to size. Glue the letters to the table for a permanent display.

37 send a message
Turn wooden blocks into drawer pulls by gluing them directly to drawers. Make the cabinet more playful with a colorful paint job.

38 say the word
Personalize a favorite photo—or create a keepsake gift—by gluing letters directly to a frame's glass. Choose a glue that's designed to adhere to both wood and glass.

39 out on a ledge
A love of letters can quickly turn into an obsession. Keep your collection from running amok by turning it into a fanciful display. Place letterpress blocks on narrow ledges along with other alphabet collectibles.

For more project details, see "Dig In" on page 56.

collections

on display

Inexpensive and easy to find, these simple items are ideal for collecting.

40 making memories Wine corks inscribed with dates and occasions are fun mementos of special events, travels, or quiet dinners for two. Collected in a large pottery or wooden bowl and displayed on a coffee table, they make unusual conversation starters.

41 on a roll For a showstopping focal point, group like items in clear glass vases from the hobby store. On this table, vintage bingo, billiard, and croquet balls share a lineup with colorful glass marbles. The result is artistic—and tidy!

42 timed right Purchase wood shelves and paint them to match your wall color. Securely install the shelves and use them to show off old timepieces. The shapes and styles are amazing, and they're readily available at secondhand shops and street fairs.

43 beachy keen For a family that enjoys summers at the shore, vintage mason jars can hold collected sand and sport paper tags to identify when and where each sample was found. The jars are arranged with shells, rocks, and coral for a seaworthy display that brings back great memories.

44 well-"urned" respect Bring a garden urn indoors and fill it with your collection. Here, large conch shells and big pieces of coral group beautifully in a container that's large enough to hold it all. To take the same idea outdoors, simply plant a bush or small tree with a woody trunk in the urn and lay down shells to cover the soil.

a yard or less

Turn even the smallest scrap leftovers into pretty home accents.

45 desk job Keep office supplies tidy with a fabric organizer. Cut two large pieces of fabric; sew pockets to the front of one of them. Place the pieces together, right sides facing, and sew three sides closed, leaving the top open. Turn right side out. Slide a piece of fusible web between the layers and press. Insert lengths of ribbon (folded in half) at each top corner and stitch the top closed. Tie the ribbons to a hanger.

46 time flies For a color-coordinated clock, stretch fabric over a small canvas and staple it to the back. Poke a hole through the center of the canvas and attach a clock kit, following the manufacturer's instructions.

47 small storage Dressing up small metal jars takes just a few snippets of fabric. Glue strips around the bases and punch circles to adorn the lids.

48 see the light Gathered fabric circles, called yo-yos, are a hot decorating trend. Glue a small one onto a large one with fabric glue. Then glue the layered yo-yos around a lampshade. Finish the look with bright ribbon glued to the bottom edge.

49 set the table Turn favorite remnants into fun place mats. For each mat, cut two 13×20-inch pieces of fabric. Place them together, wrong sides facing, with a same-size sheet of fusible batting between them. Press the layers with an iron, then stitch the mat with wavy lines. Bind the mat with strips of contrasting fabric or ribbon. Fold the strips in half, press the edges under, and then stitch onto the raw edges of the mat. For a pocket, press under the edges of a fabric square, stitch across the top, and then sew the other three sides to the mat.

(50)

50 name game Cut two 4×2½-inch fabric strips; fold and press all edges under ¼ inch. Place the pieces together, wrong sides facing, and sandwich a same-size sheet of fusible web between them. Insert the ring of a metal tag under the web along one edge; press with a hot iron. Glue rickrack to the back of the strip. To form a ring, tie the strip around the napkin with ribbon.

51 laundry list Dress clothespins with fabric to make them display-worthy. Use fabric glue to cover their tops with pretty scraps and treat the finished pieces with Diamond Glaze, which dries to a clear glasslike finish. Then glue magnets to the backs.

(49)

(51)

For more project details, see "Dig In" on page 56.

52 designer details These diminutive shadow boxes come unfinished in sets of two. Use wood glue or nails to add a length of spindle railing along the bottom and then paint each piece.

a little
left over...

Odds and ends from a home project (or a few pieces bought new at a home center) can become fun architectural accents.

53 on the ledge Use epo to top crown-molding divider blocks w[...] inexpensive plywood, then paint to create these miniature shelves.

54 mark the spot For pretty place card holders to celebrate the end of your home project, use coarse-grit sandpaper to smooth finials (if they have a dowel at the base that's part of the turned piece, simply snap it off using pliers). Use a handsaw to cut a slit for a card; paint in fun colors. Set out extras to display photos of your renovation in progress.

55 green house Create a stunning planter box using spare trim pieces. Start with a rough redwood planter and sand lightly. Glue on trim, prime and paint, and then install legs.

56 end-to-end Create stunning bookends using antique or even mismatched corbels. Can't find them at a flea market? Buy some made from composite material at a home center (as we did). Use a gouge to carve a hole in the bottom of each one and fill with fishing sinkers. Use wood filler to seal the holes, paint, and then cover the bottoms with cork or felt.

57 quick change A basic bench becomes a striking coffee table with the addition of decorative molding on the sides and a coat of bold paint.

58 on the fence Turn fence-post caps into a fun photo or picture display perfect for dressing up your front porch or interior room. Paint them and then drill holes for wire holders. Use needle-nose pliers to make interesting coils and bends in lengths of wire, then insert into the caps.

59 bold art Scraps of decorative friezes, spindles, plinth blocks, or rosettes make a statement when set off by a crisp white frame. Insert colorful scrapbook paper in the frame as a background. Then use Mirror Mastic adhesive to apply the piece directly to the frame's glass.

59

For more project details, see "Dig In" on page 56.

62

fabric
face-lifts

Check out these ideas— each using a yard of fabric or less—and get started with your own decorating redos.

60 memo board Covered in retro-inspired fabric, a stretched artist's canvas becomes a practical memo board. A sheet-metal square added to one side is magnetic for hanging bits and pieces, and the vellum calendar opposite will keep you on schedule.

61 pillow cover Give a standard pillow a fresh look by sewing an easy slipcover. Allowing enough fabric for an overlap, sew two sides together. Fold under the raw edges at the overlap. Slip the cover over the pillow and close the opening with three covered buttons.

62 decorative balls Group together fabric-covered balls to make a great filler for a bowl, a glass vase, or a basket. Cut fabric strips from coordinating fabrics and use glue to adhere the strips to plastic-foam balls. Select a variety of fabric patterns and use both small and large balls for extra interest.

63 cabinet panels Reface a pair of doors while also hiding the cabinet's contents by lining the glass panels with patterned fabric. On the back of each door, stretch the fabric over the glass and use a staple gun to fasten the edges to the wooden frame. For a tidy appearance inside, conceal the staples with glued-down coordinating ribbon.

Pick **large** patterns and bright colors for **big impact**.

Cut out a favorite **fabric element** and add it to a project.

64 glass charms Use up even the tiniest bits and pieces of leftover or favorite fabrics with these wineglass charms. Cut small squares of selected areas of the fabric and insert each into a frame pendant. Earring-hoop wire threaded through the pendant loop makes it easy to attach the charm to a wineglass stem.

65 stationery art Abstract fabric cutouts dress up plain card stock to make easy framed art. (Out of the frame, your handiwork doubles as terrific custom all-occasion greeting cards.) Gel pen outlines and a decorative scalloped edge give the cards a polished look in the frame.

66 chair cover You don't need to slipcover an entire chair to give it a fresh new look. Make this chair-back cover with just two squares of fabric and use fusible web to adhere a fabric shape to one piece. Finish with coordinating binding tape adhered to the edges with fusible web.

67 table runner Stitch a table runner by making a fabric sandwich with a piece of same-size batting in between. With right sides facing out and layers pinned together, sew straight quilting lines through all pieces along the length of it. Cover the edges with binding tape adhered with fusible web.

For more project details, see "Dig In" on page 56.

on display

Turn simple, inexpensive shadow boxes, shelves, or frames into wall art that wows.

68 sew cute Glue buttons to a box frame with silicone adhesive. Spray-paint chipboard letters and let dry. Attach the letters and a vintage needle kit with crafts glue; use silicone adhesive to adhere the spools of thread.

69 heavy metal Find vintage embossed tin ceiling tiles at flea markets or new ones at hardware stores. Cut one to fit a frame using a utility knife. Sand any rough edges, then adhere the pieces to the frame with construction-grade adhesive. Add color by brushing a thin coat of crafts paint over it. For a rustic finish, wipe the excess from raised areas.

70 get the message Frayed fabric edges create cottage charm on this simple shadow box. Tear vintage fabrics into small pieces and adhere them to the frame edges with a thin, even coat of crafts glue. Inside, use stickpins to attach a painted tree-topper and then spell out a word with board-game pieces applied with crafts glue.

71 flower power For this two-tone look, remove the glass and then apply flower decals to the front of the frame and spray-paint it. Once dry, remove the decals. Next, make a stencil for each flower center by covering the flower with painter's tape and cutting out the center with a crafts knife. When all but the centers are covered, paint the frame with a second color. Let dry. Remove the painter's tape and replace the glass.

72

73

72 in good taste **Whether it's filled with heirlooms from Grandma or just pieces found at a thrift store, this shadow box pays homage to life in the kitchen. Decoupage the frame front with original or photocopied recipe snippets. Inside, arrange utensils and bottle caps in a pleasing design and attach them with silicone adhesive or stickpins.**

73 paper chase **Vintage wallpaper lays down the charm. To give a boring mat character, cover it with old wallpaper using decoupage medium. Allow rips from piecing the paper for extra character. Attach strips of contrasting card stock to the frame edges with crafts glue, and finish the frame with another coat of decoupage medium. Layer a paper flower and a bingo card under the glass for a whimsical piece.**

more ideas

Here are five additional ways to bring life to a shadow box and showcase unusual art.

74 Glue silk flowers to the frame's edge to create a floral masterpiece. Tack a vintage seed bag to the center.

75 Decoupage playing cards to the frame's rim. On the inside, arrange dice in interesting patterns and shapes.

76 Place a favorite black and white photo on the inside and paint the frame a vibrant color such as an eye-catching red.

77 Adhere baby shoes under the glass. Use pages from a favorite baby book to cover the frame.

78 Fill the shadow box with marbles that match your home's decor. Cover the frame with fabric in a supporting color.

79 drive time Take a plain shelf out of neutral gear and head for the style fast lane by detailing it with a colorful license plate. Find an expired plate at a flea market and trim it to fit the shelf using tin snips. Soften the corners and sharp edges with a metal file and then adhere the pieces to the shelf with construction-grade adhesive.

80 shelf couture Punched-leather belts can become fashion-forward accents for a basic display ledge. Choose a matching pair or two different belts of similar color and style. Cut off the hardware using a utility knife, and then attach the pieces to the shelf with silicone adhesive. When it's dry, cover the edges and seams with leather cording adhered with crafts glue.

81 new view Topped with a slim wooden shipping crate and decorative trim, this colorful shelf looks nothing like its former self. Start by spray-painting the shelf and trim. Use a miter saw to cut the crate and trim to fit the shelf's top, and then adhere the pieces with construction-grade adhesive. Drill pilot holes for the cup hooks you add along the bottom.

more ideas

Try these other methods for turning an ordinary shelf into a masterpiece.

82 Trim brightly patterned scrapbook paper to fit the shelf.

83 Glue rows of fabric ribbon to fill the height of the ledge.

84 Fasten nailhead trim to the top and bottom of the shelf to give it an edgy look. Paint the middle in a brilliant color that complements your walls.

85 Use stencils to add life to a plain shelf. The larger the pattern, the more abstract your ledge will look.

redefined
finds

Looking for great style on the cheap? Give new life to castoffs found at flea markets and garage sales with these inspiring makeovers.

before

86 creative cigar boxes A foursome of cigar boxes becomes a pretty and practical set of stacking jewelry boxes with a coordinated palette of pale paint colors, stenciled motifs, and button accents. Add feet to each box with gilded wooden balls glued to the bottom corners.

87 lucky lampshade Remove the covering from a lampshade and spray-paint the frame. Trace each side of the frame onto a place mat, cut out the pieces, and punch holes along the edges with a hammer and nail. Thread wire through the holes and twist it around the frame to secure.

88 flee the nest A dab of paint is all you need to achieve the cloudlike look on the tops of these nesting tables. After painting the legs and sides a solid color, apply thinned paint to the tabletop using a sea sponge in a dabbing motion. Repeat with two or three more colors and feather the edges. Seal the top with polyurethane.

89 desk job Because of a redo years before, the dark finish and shabby doors on this drop-down desk made it less than appealing. But a fresh coat of taupe paint on the exterior and a splash of light blue on the cubbies give it a brand-new look.

90 ottoman redo With a tapered form and tufted top, this ottoman only needed fresh batting and upholstery. Textured bath towels stretched over the batting and stapled in place fill that last bill on a budget. Casters screwed to the bottom make it portable.

before

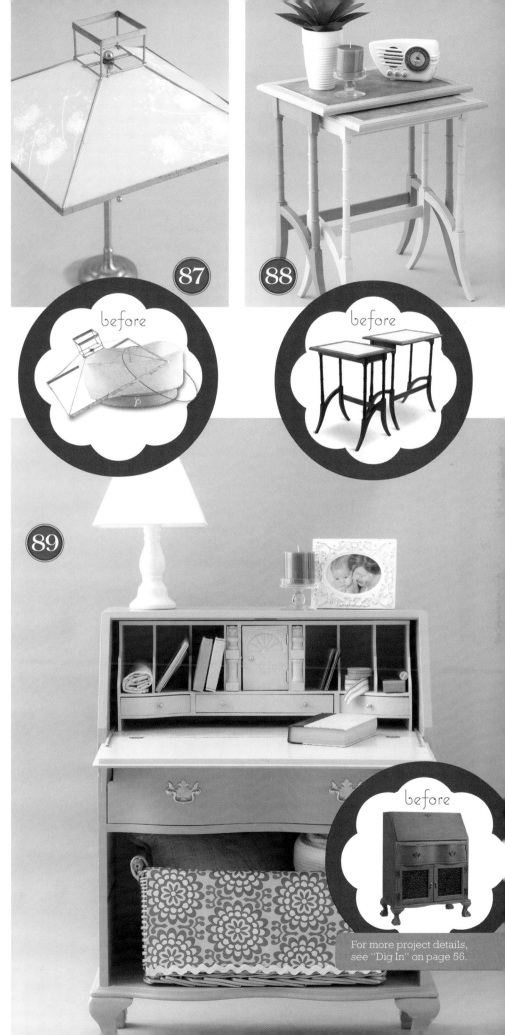

before

before

before

For more project details, see "Dig In" on page 56.

find it...
use it!

91

Small objects tossed in the garbage heap get a new lease on life. Here's how to do it.

FOR YOU

91 down the drain A wire dish drainer takes on a fresh outlook after an age-defying coat of white spray paint. Now the slots cradle office supplies. Slip in a jar to hold pens and brushes. When searching flea markets for a drainer, make sure it will work with the items you wish to store (large folders may require taller supports).

92 light bright A decorative light fixture is the perfect perch for a candle. Coat it with metallic paint and place your new candleholder on a saucer to protect the tabletop from damage.

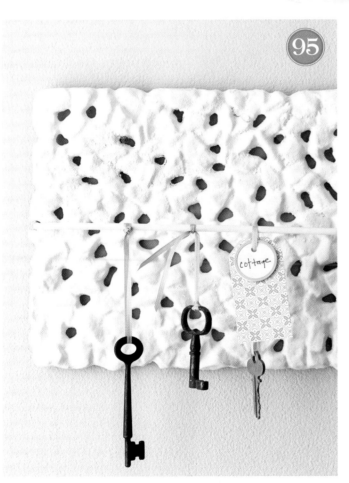

93 make a splash Separated from its base, this concrete birdbath already wears the beautiful patina of age. To make it room-ready, simply scrub the basin with disinfectant soap. When it's dry, place it on a table and fill with shells or other collectibles. You'll likely want to adhere a piece of felt on the bottom to protect your surface.

94 put a spin on it Take your coffee table for a drive by bolting vintage wheels to the legs. To attach them, drill through the legs and insert bolts into the wheel hubs. Slide the bolts through the legs and secure with nuts. Make sure to buy a matching set of wheels for smooth moving.

95 rack 'em up An old iron grate with a simple handle makes a great spot for hanging keys. Thread a ribbon through the keys to hang them, or for removable storage, use S hooks instead. The holes in the grate make it easy to attach to a wall.

For more project details, see "Dig In" on page 56.

attitude-adjusted

Castoffs with good lines make great makeover projects. Just look at these five inspiring examples.

96

96 in the chest
A good scrubbing improves any cast-off piece, but that's only the first step in this redo. A new breed of wallpaper, one that's vinyl-free and peels off, makes this project fun for now and easy to change later. If you choose a simple linen-look wallpaper like this, we promise you'll be able to move the piece to any room in the house.

97 leather-wrapped chair
Chairs are surprising bargains at flea markets and furniture outlets. Look for one with an interesting shape; then give it a stylish makeover using paint and faux leather. Faux leather, a vinyl product, can be cut to any shape and won't ravel. That makes it perfect for wrapping around seats or gluing to curved surfaces.

98 steel-topped table
This classic wicker table looks ready for the den with its handsome new finish and top. The finish is leather dye rubbed over the worn paint. The top, made from 20-gauge cold-rolled steel, is both hardworking and stylish. Best of all, this refurbished table can move easily from a country home to one in the city.

99 lost your marbles
Glass and silver work their magic on this once brown and boring mirror. The silver comes from paint that hides the old finish, and the glass arrives via three rows of clear marbles glued to the mirror's surface. The trick is to use a clear industrial-strength crafts adhesive to ensure that the marbles stay put.

100 fabric update
Imagine a sideboard for the dining room that's as easy to update as changing a tablecloth. That's the strategy behind this dressy makeover. The piece, painted in go-with-anything black, features fabric panels that slip into place on the serving surface and bottom shelf. The covering is adhered to fusible fabric backing, so there's no sewing required. Simply cut, fuse, and enjoy.

For more project details, see "Dig In" on page 56.

TABLE *talk*

With a keen eye, you can spot a potentially pretty table at a flea market or even in your own basement. All you need is a flat surface and some creativity.

101 on a roll If you've retired your croquet set, make use of its colorful mallets for a clever family room coffee table. Start with two old window screens and add large casters to one for a base. Remove the mallet handles and glue and screw the mallet heads between the two screens. Top the rolling table with a piece of glass—ask the glass shop to seam the edges for safety.

THE GOLDEN BOOK ENCYCLOPEDIA

102 urban chic Take liberties with inexpensive basics to create beautiful and functional furniture. Here, an upside-down galvanized bucket combined with a glass tabletop makes a funky coffee table.

103 seaside surface Guests will go wild over this serving table made from old water skis. Securely fasten the skis to the top of weather-beaten ladders and planks. Use the table to display Thermos vases, a vintage cooler, and all the drinks and snacks you'll need for a hungry crowd.

104 wave reviews Visit a salvage shop and you'll likely see piles of old porch-post molds. Though they're rounded on the inside, they're flat on the outside. For this end table, mount the mold to an old fern stand. Drill through the inside of the mold and into the stand, cover the screws with sand, add seashells, and top with glass.

105 garden style Craft a cute see-through table to display vintage garden treasures—top a birdbath with glass. If necessary, use epoxy to hold the top and bottom of the birdbath together. Look for an inexpensive precut piece of glass at a home-decor store.

106 different beat You don't need a drummer in the family to add beat to your living room. Purchase a vintage cocktail drum on eBay or at a flea market, and convert it to an unforgettable end table by cutting a piece of glass to fit the top.

107 clever cubbies Scoop up old post-office cubbies to make a wine rack with character. Line the bottom of each opening with coordinating scrapbook papers. Paint wooden legs in a matching color and attach them to the bottom.

haute handcrafts

All grown up and perfect for quick designs, felt isn't just for Girl Scout projects anymore.

108 unify a design Draw together a room's colors with coasters made from circles of felt in different sizes. Use a die-cutting tool for the shapes or pattern your own. Tack the pieces together with simple stitches of embroidery floss, adding beads to the stitches for decoration.

Felted wool makes decorating **a snap.** Cut felt won't fray, so you can create an **intricate** design without the fuss of finishing edges.

109 add dimension

Café curtains do the trick, but they often lack personality. Dress up yours with precut motifs. Fabric glue secures the pieces in place. Can't find precut pieces? Make your own using a die-cutting tool found at most scrapbook stores.

110 make a statement

Handmade art is in vogue, so get crafty with purchased felt leaf shapes that you mount in shadow boxes with scrapbook-paper mats. Decorative stick pins and snips of ribbon complete the look.

111 add texture
Throw pillows can change the vibe of a room in an instant. This one is made from various colors of wool felt pieced together. An added bonus: Felt doesn't fray, so the edges are left rough-cut.

112 on the run
A table runner adds a touch of style to any surface—and they're usually under $10. Add a custom design with an intricately cut self-adhesive felt design from a crafts store.

113 personal touch
Use special pillow shams in a guest bedroom. Sew them from wool felt. Print out your guest's initial, trace it onto felt, and cut it out. Back with a piece of complementary fabric.

For more project details, see "Dig In" on page 56.

today's chalkboard

114 got the time Keep track of the time and important reminders on a clock with a chalkboard-paint face-lift. Use a purchased wooden clock and carefully remove the hands before painting. After the paint is dry, replace the hands and write numbers and messages on the face.

115 multicolor dresser Black paint may evoke memories of blackboards in grade school, but these drawer fronts get a colorful treatment with pastel shades of chalkboard paint. Write labels on the drawers and you'll know at a glance what's inside.

Chalk it up to nostalgia or practicality—the chalkboard look is making a comeback. Paint and repositionable vinyl decals make it easy to add to your decorating mix.

116 talkative table runner A clever addition to a buffet or dinner table, this chalkboard table runner (made from oilcloth) is a creative spot for writing messages. Bind the edges with ribbon and double-sided fabric tape for a colorful finish.

117 game time Give a plain tabletop a winning touch with a coat of chalkboard paint. Game lovers will appreciate being able to keep score or play favorite childhood games such as tic-tac-toe directly on the table.

more ideas

The uses for chalkboard paint are virtually limitless. Here are two more ideas.

119 Coat the inside of a cabinet door with chalkboard paint so you can scribble your grocery list, keep track of your to-dos, and jot reminders to yourself.

120 Keep the playroom tidy by painting squares of chalkboard paint on storage bins and labeling them with the correct belongings.

118 cookie jar You don't need paint to get the chalkboard look on this jar. Just trim repositionable vinyl chalkboard to the desired size, round the corners with a punch, and stick it on.

122

feather
your nest

Do a little bird-watching in your bath with motifs borrowed from nature.

121

121 sweet and simple Turn a soap dish into a pretty accessory by nestling it in a crafts-store twig nest. Fill it with egg-shaped soaps. For a wall-mounted soap holder to match your towel bar, attach a sturdy piece of limb where it forks to the wall and hot-glue the nest in place.

122 branch out Turn a tree limb into a one-of-a-kind towel rack. Choose a branch that's sturdy and disease-free and mount it to the wall with brackets for lightweight hand towels. For heavier towels, choose a thicker branch.

123 avian artwork Turn inexpensive paper coasters into instant framed art. Spot-glue the coasters to colorful card stock (or use double-stick tape) and mount them in off-the-shelf frames. Look for square shadow boxes at your crafts store to give the thick coasters definition.

124 get a handle Make a big impression on guests when you decorate a handled pail—it takes less than a minute— with a giant graphic sticker. Fill the pail with bath essentials that move easily from the sink to the tub.

125 wing it Embellish hand towels (or even dinner napkins) with a freehand drawing of an egg using fabric pens. Rubber-stamp a bird image on colorful card stock or cut out an image from a note card to tie around each towel. If you're computer savvy, print images from clip art.

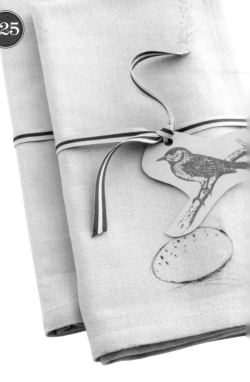

to the
letter

A letter (or two or three) that symbolizes your name is beautiful in any context. Give rooms personal style by using your monogram on all manner of home furnishings.

126 top off a table

Add sophistication to your table with monogrammed place mats and napkins. Determine where dishes will sit on the place mat and how you'll fold the napkins. Then stencil or embroider lettering onto the fabric in a spot where it will get the best display.

127 table the contents Give plain plates special-occasion character. Use a computer and color printer to make oversize ampersands or exclamation points. Copy them onto waterslide decal paper (a reverse image will appear), cut around the motifs, and follow the manufacturer's instructions to apply them to the plate. Finish with a food-safe spray varnish to protect against scratching and fading. For napkins, print memorable quotes on iron-on transfer paper and transfer them to cotton or cotton-blend fabrics.

128 perk up a pillow Make a bold statement on a purchased pillow with one large letter. We used a "K" in Castellar type and asked an online custom-stencil site to send us the precut Mylar letter. To apply the paint, remove the pillow form and place a flat piece of cardboard inside to keep the paint from bleeding through. Replace the pillow form after the paint dries.

129 be seated New cushions and slipcovers can completely transform the look of a dining space. Slip them on and off whenever the occasion warrants. Make them more personal by stenciling a monogram and border on the back of each one. We used the Harrington font and cut our own stencil. You also can find large, beautiful alphabet stencils at crafts and hobby stores.

130 personalize a planter

Flank your front door with a pair of stenciled planters. Use your monogram or opt for house numbers instead. Coat the planter with primer and then apply a base-coat color. Over the top, sponge on one or two shades of lighter paint. If at any time the painted surface feels rough, lightly sand with fine-grit sandpaper before going on to the next step. Stencil on your design and finish with a coat of varnish.

131 sleep on it

In this bedroom, a weathered mantel stands in for a pricey headboard. On top, the homeowners' initials, given to them as a wedding gift, double as artwork. Watch for old display lettering at antiques shows and markets. Look for new examples at home-decorating stores and online. If the sizes aren't the same, all the better—variety makes the display interesting.

132 serve up style

Paint a large wooden tray for your next party. The flat surface provides the perfect canvas for your creativity. Give the tray one coat of primer and two coats of paint. Lightly sand after the primer to ensure a smooth paint application. Decorate the tray with an oversize Edwardian-script monogram (get one custom-cut at **stencilplanet.com**) surrounded by a wreath motif from a purchased stencil. Add two coats of varnish for durability.

133 earn an "a" Use painted wooden lettering to accent shelves. In bookcases, line the backs with wallpaper to make art and accessories stand out. Cut the paper to size, test the fit, and then coat the wallpaper with paste before smoothing it into place.

pages

8–9 Hidden Gems

Mass-produced costume jewelry first became popular in the 1930s, when difficult economic times led women to seek out more affordable accessories. Made of inexpensive materials such as rhinestones and brass, some pieces are replicas of expensive heirlooms while others are just colorful, oversize, fun, and playful.

Though its origins may be humble, costume jewelry is now a collector's item, with particular interest in Bakelite and Art Deco–inspired pieces. Prices vary widely. Find affordable reproduction designs at **luckylooloo.com** and **emitations.com.** For vintage pieces, take your chances on eBay and buy a large bag filled with random items for as little as a few dollars. Or spend $20 to $100 on one perfect piece at **vintagecostumejewels.com,** which is searchable by color, era, or materials.

pages

18–19 On the Map

Get a grip

Look for unconventional items that can be used as drawer pulls for a chest of drawers. These miniature globes were vending-machine prizes bought in bulk on eBay and fitted with a screw through a drilled hole.

You can turn most anything into a clock. Shop online for battery-operated clock kits that include movements and hands.

pages

20–21 Type Casting

Buy the Letter

Long ago replaced by word processing software and digital printers, wooden printing blocks—once used to transfer designs or characters to paper—are now hot collector's items. Printing blocks come in several sizes and fonts. Here are a few of our favorite online resources:

* **eBay.com (search "printing block")**
* **Etsy.com (search "vintage letterpress block")**
* **Three Potato Four, threepotatofourshop.com**

pages
24–25 A Yard or Less

Sew Simple

A perennial favorite among quilters, a fabric yo-yo is a gathered circle secured with a simple running stitch. The cute designs can be used as accents on anything from clothes to lampshades or sewn together to make a quilt. To make, cut a circle about twice the size you want to end up with and then follow these simple steps:

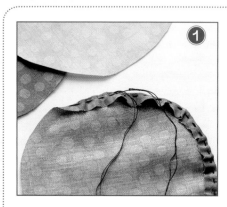

1. Begin to Stitch
Fold under ¼ inch of fabric. Thread a needle with sturdy 100-percent-cotton thread and knot the end. Take small, evenly spaced running stitches near the folded edge all the way around the circle. Bigger stitches will allow the fabric to gather more.

2. Tighten the Thread
End your stitching just next to the starting point; don't cut the thread. Gently pull the thread end to gather the folded edge until it forms a gathered circle. The right side of the fabric will develop soft pleats as you gather the edge. Take a small stitch to hold the gathers in place, then knot your thread and cut off the end. Take a backstitch over the knot so it doesn't pull out.

3. Sew Yo-Yos Together
To join yo-yos, place them with gathered fronts together. Using matching thread, whipstitch them together for about ½ inch. Make rows of joined yo-yos, then sew together the rows in the same way. When stitching yo-yos together, use small stitches that won't show prominently.

pages
26–29 A Little Left Over ...

Create character

Architectural salvage shops are opening in cities across the country. If your town doesn't have one yet, you can find interesting and reclaimed materials online at these sites:

- **vandykes.com**
- **rensup.com**
- **classicdetails.com**

pages
30–33 Fabric Face-Lifts

An *expert tip*...
Cutting out a portion of fabric, such as a flower or other design element, is known as fussy cutting.

upclose

No-Sew Solution

For a no-sew fabric embellishment, use fusible web to apply fabric shapes to a larger fabric background. Look for heavyweight paper-backed fusible web at the fabrics store.

Here's how to use it:

1. Cut a piece of fusible web approximately ¼ inch larger on all sides than the desired fabric motif.

2. Place the fusible web, paper side up, on the wrong side of the designated fabric, centering it over the desired motif. Following the manufacturer's instructions, press in place; let cool.

3. Cut out the fabric motif as desired. Note: You don't need to leave any seam allowances as fused edges will not be turned under. Peel off the paper backing.

4. Place the fused fabric motif onto the fabric background, fusible-web side down. Press in place.

pages
38–39 Redefined Finds

before

inside

Transform this old desk into a beauty with a coat of fresh paint.

You've found the perfect piece of furniture. Time to paint, right? Hold on. Always sand and prime painted furniture before repainting with a fresh coat. Sanding with medium-grit sandpaper will give the new paint "tooth," or a rough surface to adhere to. Applying primer helps to conceal the old paint—that way you'll save time and money with fewer coats of the new paint color.

pages
40–41 Find It ... Use It!

Put your imagination to work when strolling the aisles of a flea market. These well-worn objects grabbed our attention. For their "happily ever after" photos, see *pages 40–41*.

Try these online flea market bargain spots!

✳ **furnituretrader.com**
✳ **greatstuffbypaul.com**
✳ **oldandsold.com**
✳ **qflea.com**
✳ **rubylane.com**

before

pages

42–43 Attitude-Adjusted

Shop flea markets for makeover projects!

To find flea markets in your area, use an Internet search engine and type in flea markets/location. You're likely to turn up several where you live or plan to travel.

Fine Finishing

Try these two projects. See close-up images *below*.

1. Add patina to a steel tabletop:

✱ Clean the surface with soap and water.

✱ Spray the surface with vinegar; let set overnight. The surface will rust and discolor. Clean; repeat the vinegar treatment two more times.

✱ Apply furniture wax at regular intervals to maintain the finish.

2. Finish the fabric for a sideboard top:

✱ Cut fusible fabric backing to fit the sideboard top and shelf.

✱ Iron damask fabric onto the fusible backing, leaving 2 inches of fabric around all edges; follow package instructions. Trim damask fabric ½ inch larger than the fusible fabric.

✱ Fold the damask to the back of the fusible fabric; press.

✱ Use heat-activated fabric webbing to bond the damask to the back of the fusible fabric; follow package directions.

pages

46–47 Haute Handcrafts

An expert tip...

Turn a wool sweater into felt by washing it on the hot wash/cold rinse cycle several times.

Shape up

Felt is great for repetitive-pattern art. Look around the house for pattern-making materials such as cookie cutters, juice cans, soda cans, jewelry boxes, antique plates, flowerpots, fluted vases, stencils, and paperweights.

Rings true

Use up your felt scraps with this quick and easy idea. Cut the remnants into 6-inch-long strips and add felt embellishments with fabric glue. Close the strip into a circle using fabric glue or hook-and-loop tape stitched in place on the ends.

create

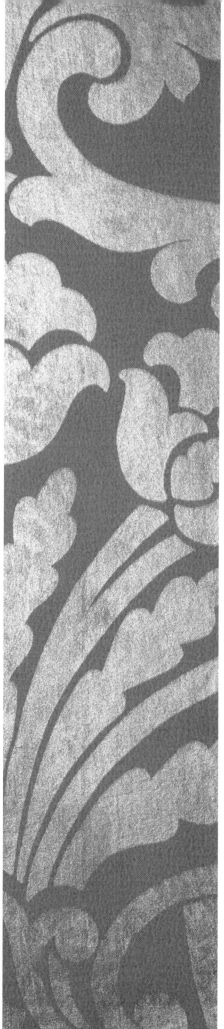

cottage
retreat

Pile on the charm in a sun-filled sitting room by fashioning decorative projects made from vintage fabrics and secondhand finds.

134 get the message
Serve up notes in style on a metal tray turned message board. Prime and paint the tray and then turn vintage buttons into pretty message holders by hot-gluing a bit of magnetic tape to their backs.

135 hang time Vintage pillowcases often have pretty borders. To turn them into café curtains, fold the top of the case to the back so the bottom skims the window ledge when it's hanging.

136 granny chic To make wicker chairs indoor destinations, paint them a bright color and layer on cushions and pillows made from vintage bedspreads. Use an extra-deep cushion on the seat for stay-awhile comfort.

137 for the dogs Honor your favorite pet with this easy project. Make a color photocopy of a quilt section and then trace a silhouette onto the paper and cut it out. Secure the image with double-sided tape.

138 table topper This petite side table is actually an old metal stool topped with a picture frame. To make it, glue or screw the frame to a circle of plywood, and then screw the plywood to the stool top. Hide the screw heads by decoupaging paper to the plywood.

139 fork it over Artwork easels can be hard to find in diminutive sizes. Solve the dilemma by making your own out of vintage forks. Use them to showcase greeting cards or small pieces of art.

140 case closed Turn a beat-up hutch into display-worthy storage. Attach wooden feet to the bottom to raise the cabinet off the floor. Sand, prime, and paint the piece. Let it dry, then add new latches and glass pulls. Wallpaper the cabinet's back and lower door panels with vintage scraps.

141 underfoot Turn a wooden hat box into a storage ottoman by adding small casters and a cushion fashioned from an old yo-yo pillow snagged at a flea market. Secure the cushion to the lid with carpet tape or heavy-duty hook-and-loop tape.

Piece together **pretty sections** from an **old quilt** to make sweet accent pillows.

142 pet project This adorable pillow is the cat's meow. Cut the pieces using the pattern on *page 118* in "Dig In." Sew wrong sides together, starting with the tail pieces. Stuff the tail and sew closed. As you're sewing the body pieces together, sew the tail into the back seam. Sew closed, and finish it off by hand sewing the tail to the front.

143 top design Cap a window with a valance made from medium-density fiberboard (MDF). Cut the sides and front to fit your window and use a jigsaw to make a scallop along the bottom edge. Screw the pieces together, and then wallpaper the finished box.

For more project details, see "Dig In" on page 118.

amazing as is

ROOT BEER

ROOT BEER

Don't pass up great bargains in the as-is pile. Use them to give your space a blast from the past.

144 top shelf A to-do list can be a beautiful thing. For this message center, mount a small shelf to a vintage cabinet door. Cover the inset panel in chalkboard paint with a magnetic additive.

145 around the yard Use a hand saw to miter sections of old yardsticks, creating colorful and graphic photo mats that turn basic frames into works of art.

146 bin-tin-tin Corral crafts supplies and infuse vintage charm into your room in a three-tiered stand made from salvaged tins.

147 poetic license Use tin snips to cut apart old license plates and create a memorable address marker. Use Liquid Nails to attach the pieces to salvaged lumber.

148 serving up style Put mismatched silverware to work as photo or card holders. Place a piece of floral foam in the bottom of a flowerpot, insert the fork handle into the foam, and cover the base with floral moss. Use pliers to curl the prongs.

Transforming a discard into a one-of-a-kind decorative accent isn't just creative fun, it's also an **earth-friendly** alternative to buying new.

149 smokin' storage Store recipe cards or small odds and ends in cigar-box bins. Add drawer pulls to the boxes and stash them on a ledge or in an old produce crate outfitted with plywood shelves.

150 costumed comfort Turn vintage clothes into a shabby chic accessory. Cut squares from old shirts, sandwiching trim between them. With right sides facing, sew the pieces together, leaving an opening to turn; turn right side out. Cut different-size circles from complementary fabrics, pin them together, and attach to the pillow with a brooch. Insert a pillow form and hand-stitch the opening closed.

151 sweet light Crafted from wire fencing and Chinese lantern bulbs, this chandelier will make a statement over the dining table or at your next garden party.

For more project details, see "Dig In" on page 118.

sleep on it

Invoke sweet slumber with a bedroom sanctuary filled with secondhand objects turned first-rate accessories. These eight ideas will get you started.

153

152

153 shaker vases These diminutive shakers have found new life as vases for pretty little nosegays. Remove the caps and insert short-stemmed flowers into each milky-white container. Then display the collection in a row on a shelf made from vintage door molding.

152 porch pairing Retire a pair of old porch posts from their hardworking past by using them as a decorative headboard. Mounted on either side of the mattress, the tall distressed posts provide a feeling of substance. Frame a favorite piece of fabric with an oval white mat, and mount it between the posts for a centerpiece.

154

155

156

157

158

154 linen chest An old bead-board chest dons a fresh coat of aqua paint to tie into the cottage-style color scheme of the bedroom. Lined with lively fabric stapled to the interior, the chest practically begs to be left open.

155 hanging storage Keep magazines and books within arm's reach by storing them in a vintage bucket that hangs from a plant hook by the bedside.

156 table conversion An ideal space-saving accent, this drop-leaf table was transformed into one half its size with a few simple cuts. Paint the "drop" side of the table and mount it to the wall to create a demilune with two original legs attached underneath.

157 glass stack Short on candleholders? Make your own by gathering a variety of glass plates and bowls, stacking them in an interesting way, and topping your creation with a fragrant candle.

158 fabric art Gather a few of your favorite fabrics and showcase them in an assortment of mismatched frames.

159 on the table This vintage table doubles as a desk and a bedside stand. To soften the look for the bedroom, cover the top with fabric and fasten it along the edges with upholstery tacks.

159

For more project details, see "Dig In" on page 118.

recycled
chic

If you know where to look, you can unearth treasures at every turn in an antiques mall. This casually elegant room proves it.

160

161 grate artwork Ironworkers of the past took pride in creating intricate patterns in metal, even on ordinary grates. You can find these artistic examples at any flea market, antiques shop, or farm auction. Though many collectors use them as tabletops, both indoors and out, here they make a statement displayed on a shelf.

160 going green A comfortable and structurally sound but otherwise ordinary chair steals the spotlight in this room. Painted a bolder shade of lime than the walls, the chair adds needed punch. Once you find a chair that works in your space, glue any loose joints and clean it thoroughly. After applying a coat of quality primer, finish with two coats of your accent color.

162 made for media This old office credenza was dark, damaged, and boring, but it had great bones. With a fresh coat of white primer followed by white paint, it's right at home in this living room. What lends the new media center its "wow" factor, however, are the bright red painted doors and striped fabric panels.

163 garden center Using a tall plant stand and a handled tool caddy, create an indoor window box. From inside the box, screw the two pieces together. To keep water from spilling onto the rug and floor, use pots with no drainage holes. (Drainage holes aren't critical if you can control the amount of water each plant gets.)

164 around the globe Vintage globes often end up at salvage yards when they become outdated. Use them to dress up counters and add a bit of sophistication to any room.

165 the panel is in For one-of-a-kind, easy-sew curtains, dress the bottoms of purchased panels with vintage tablecloths. Cut a tablecloth in half and sew it to the bottom edge of a curtain, easing it to fit with small gathers or pleats if necessary.

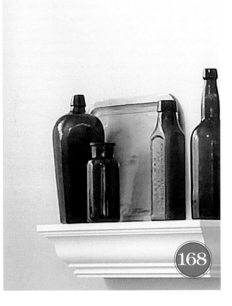

166 clever storage A chicken feeder's length is an ideal CD holder. When shopping for antiques, follow your heart when you see something that speaks to you. Once you get it home, you'll find a spot for it.

167 wired for remote No longer in service, this wire dish drainer makes a great coffee-table basket for books, papers, and elusive remote controls.

168 colorful collections Add interest to your room by grouping collections on shelves and table surfaces. On a small shelf above the display, amber bottles counterbalance the weight of the large media storage unit.

169 pillow placeholder Use a wire basket to corral pillows and keep your space looking clutter-free.

170 pieces of the past Make a large coffee table by piecing together a collection of wooden items. Start at the bottom with a furniture-mover's dolly made from medium-density fiberboard (MDF). Then add wooden crates, and top it all off with a well-worn barn door.

171 a little fishy Transform any large bowl into a home for your fish. Here, a fishbowl sits on top of the coffee table, adding life to the living room.

172 egg-centric lighting
Inspire guests to relax and ask questions by turning an old wire egg basket into a lampshade. Line the sides with fabric and turn it upside down on the lamp base.

173 perfect marriage
Adding a 24-inch-round piece of painted plywood turns a fern stand into a quaint end table. Get the same look by using a precut wooden tabletop from your home center. Once you've painted and aged it with antiquing medium, attach it to the stand.

174 trompe l'oeil art Fool the eye with a stenciled design painted right on the wall and topped with a frame. Decide where you'll hang the frame before applying the paint—there's no moving this.

beachy
keen

Whether you live near the water or just wish you did, give your home seaside style with these ideas for turning flea market finds into oceanside-inspired accents.

175

176

178 a step up Retired ladders can do more than hold quilts. By adding old vent grates to each rung (simply screw them in place), you extend storage space and add vintage charm.

175 art smart Let colorful tablecloths fill in for expensive artwork. This project is perfect for stained cloths that would otherwise wind up in the trash. Hot-glue a starfish over one of the cloths for dimension.

176 seaside chic The original orange table and gray bench didn't scream seaside chic. To update the rescued furniture, we painted the table sandy yellow and the bench ocean blue. To finish the makeover, we added starfish stencils around the apron.

177 bottled up A painted runner tops off the revamped dining table. It backdrops a collection of sand and rocks gathered during family vacations displayed in a hodgepodge of vintage-glass jars.

179 with this ring Add simple details to your table for a chic custom look. To dress up basic metal napkin rings, simply use hot glue to attach pieces of sea glass found at the beach.

180 have a seat Mismatched furniture is a hallmark of flea market style. Here, Windsor chairs sit alongside ladder-back chairs and a bench. To unite the pieces, use the same color chair cushions topped with squares cut from old tablecloths.

181 center of attention Finding weathered and unusual pieces such as this old chicken feeder is part of the fun of shopping at flea markets. The long and narrow feeder serves as a centerpiece that holds medicine bottles filled with flowers.

For more project details, see "Dig In" on page 118.

budget *beauty*

A designer bedroom with high-end touches isn't always in the budget. Here, it's re-created at a fraction of the price.

182

183

184

185

The inspiration bedroom spotted in *Decorating* magazine cost thousands of dollars, while ours was just hundreds.

182 stolen tones The first step in bringing our room to life was stealing the original color palette. To get the look just right, a home center color-matched the wall and furniture paints from the magazine story.

183 head of the class An upholstered headboard can be affordable if you use medium-density fiberboard (MDF) as the base and cover it with ordinary canvas dressed up with fabric-covered buttons.

184 on a roll Our version of the inspiration room's bolster pillows is simple. Fold a hand towel in half lengthwise and sew each corner in 1 inch. Pin a fabric circle into each end and sew in place.

185 reversible throw The two-tone throw in the original bedroom was too expensive for our budget, but we got a similar look by attaching a fabric square to the back of a solid throw with buttons.

186 trophy case The lamps in the original bedroom reminded us of trophies. We found a silver trophy at an online auction and turned it into a lamp using a kit from a home center.

187 mat magic Custom matting is pricey. To get a similar look for our artwork, we covered the mat that came with our frame with inexpensive fabric.

188 mirror, mirror Inspired by 1920s glamour, mirror-covered furniture is super trendy—and super pricey. For an affordable alternative, we painted a thrift-store dresser and had a hardware store cut mirrors to fit our dresser's drawers and attached them with mirror glue. You'll want to pay extra for polished edges if kids will be using it.

189 curtain call Shower curtains can save you big bucks on window treatments. To make this curtain fit our window, we added a panel of coordinating fabric along the bottom edge, hid the seam with ribbon, and hung the panel with ribbon ties. To make this a no-sew project, we used fusible web on all the seams.

190 details, details Turning a plain pillow into a piece of art is as simple as adding a few cents' worth of ribbon. Lay the ribbon in an interesting design, pin it in place, and attach it with fusible web.

For more project details, see "Dig In" on page 118.

better than ever

Give your living room a fresh look without spending a fortune using these low-cost, big-impact ideas.

before

191 speak volumes Make a personal statement on your walls with a rub-on quote (we created this custom design at **wonderfulgraffiti.com**). Set off the saying with matching picture frames.

Life isn't a matter of mile

s but of moments.
-Rose Fitzgerald Kennedy

192 new view
Before, this room looked old
and tired. Now simple
modern furniture makes the
space feel fresh while
accent pieces with
traditional features, like an
arch-front bookcase, keep
the look livable.

193 serve up style Make a decorative plate using waterslide decal paper. Print your design on decal paper and let the ink dry for 30 minutes. Soak the decal in water for one minute and position it on a plate, gently smoothing away air bubbles with your fingertips. When the plate is dry, apply two coats of oil-base polyurethane with a foam brush. The decal's white background will become clear as the polyurethane dries.

194 stencil savvy If wallpaper is too permanent for you, use an oversize stencil to add pattern to your walls. A mottled finish gives this damask design dimension and texture.

195 awesome overhaul Nabbed for $15 at a thrift shop, this dresser went through a dramatic transformation. After it was scrubbed clean with a bleach solution, the piece was sanded and repainted. A stencil and new hardware complete the makeover.

196 royal treatment Tone-on-tone damask curtain panels frame the window seat, adding another layer of softness to the pillow-plumped spot. The casual Roman shade diffuses light and provides a bit of privacy at night.

197 face it Immortalize family members with easy-to-make silhouette pillows. Use contrasting fabric colors for a bold statement.

198 space planning Outfitting the space under a window seat with cubbies creates a focal point. To protect from pets and sunlight, use stain- and fade-resistant fabrics on window-seat cushions.

197

198

For more project details, see "Dig In" on page 118.

light and bright

Turn your living room into a sunshine showcase. On these pages, we use quick projects and colorful decor to create a showstopping summer look.

199 modern motif By painting the bump-out wall a fresh seafoam green, the fireplace becomes the room's focal point.

200 on display A mantel above the fireplace adds depth and functionality. Made of white-painted plywood, the floating shelf displays pretty glass bottles.

201 in pieces Sectional seating is nothing if not flexible. Reconfigure the pieces with your mood for an entirely new look.

202 get inspired Making over a room can be overwhelming. Simplify the process by finding one inspirational piece to guide your redesign. For example, a graphic green-and-white tablecloth (now a curtain panel) served as the jumping-off point here.

203 square deal Carpet tiles are a fun and practical alternative to an area rug. Different colors or motifs can be arranged and rearranged in creative designs, like this cream-and-seafoam checkered pattern.

204 pillow play Making pillows is a snap when you use a two-ply place mat as your fabric. Cut a slit along the top back of the mat and stuff with batting, leaving the top few inches empty. Fold over and secure with a button.

205 table decor Have fun with a glass-topped bistro table by adding words and designs made from chipboard letters and stickers found in the scrapbooking aisle. Update the sentiments and designs each season.

206 cover up Hang square napkins with photo clips to create your own café curtains. The clips are hot-glued in place on window moldings.

207 on the hook Add architectural interest to a room with makeshift wainscoting. Get the look by hanging store-bought coat racks end-to-end around the room.

208 take a seat Add color to dining chairs with seat covers made from dish towels. Simply stitch ribbon ties to the towels to hold them in place.

For more project details, see "Dig In" on page 118.

vintage beauty

Search flea markets for one-of-a-kind pieces to add personality to your kitchen.

209

209 rustic wood Add character to a new kitchen with a display shelf atop the window. This ledge is made from a length of wood, two corbels, and decorative turnings glued and nailed to the shelf edge. Secure the shelf to the wall using anchor bolts. Stretch a tension rod between the corbels to hang a valance made from a tablecloth.

210 tin tiles Camouflage a refrigerator with faux tin tiles from a home center. You can use ordinary scissors to cut them to fit.

211 darling drawer pulls Add a flea market touch to new stools with vintage drawer pulls screwed into the back.

212 clever chair legs

Search for pieces such as this chair base in the "as is" section of a flea market. For a creative towel holder, cut the base apart to space the rungs away from a cabinet; then paint and install. Attach the piece by drilling through the cabinet from the inside and into the legs.

212

213 tablecloth A $24
tablecloth provides fabric for a valance and a sink skirt.

213

214 under the table
Whether they're needed for support or are purely decorative, wooden corbels work hard under an island or bar. Expect to pay more for a matched set. If you plan to use the corbels to support the weight of a counter, make sure the wood is still sound.

215 decorative window
Create an oversize tray using a window and legs made from a spindle cut into quarters. For extra strength, screw a small piece of ¼-inch plywood to the underside of each corner where the legs attach. Seal the peeling paint with polyurethane, and top the window with glass cut to size.

216 box & beakers
Keep salt and pepper handy for the cook but out of sight for diners in a carved box. Add 2 inches of rice to the box; then nestle filled glass votive holders into the rice.

217 rustic tools
Keep recipes handy with holders made from a potato masher and a meat tenderizer. Attach a clothespin or metal clip to the handles with epoxy.

218 bright bowl
To make a funky fruit bowl, turn a glass light fixture upside down, attach the bowl to a wooden base with epoxy, and pile on the produce.

For more project details, see "Dig In" on page 118.

219

pretty dining

From the grand chandelier overhead to the tiny details on the table, the projects in this room make every meal memorable.

220

219 crowning achievement Give your chandelier a new look by switching out some of the clear crystals for colored prisms. Cover the lampshades with a bold-pattern fabric, and edge them with fringe. Most crafts stores sell self-adhesive lampshade kits that include a template for cutting fabric or paper to cover shades.

220 copycat vases Fill three vases about half full with small stones before adding water and fresh peonies. Off-season, look for fresh flowers at your grocery store or ask your florist to order them for you. You also can buy quality silk versions that would fool even Mother Nature.

221 crowd-pleasers Greet your luncheon or dinner guests with a lovely place setting topped with a surprise package. Buy takeout boxes at crafts stores, place a treasure inside, and wrap ribbon around the box and tape at the bottom. Stamp a butterfly on colored paper, cut it out, and fold it in the center. Then tape it to the box top.

222 layered linens Work wonders on a simple white tablecloth by layering on hemmed lengths of fabric, first across the table and then down the center. Playing with more than one pattern is an easy way to work in all the colors in your palette. Machine-stitch a narrow hem along all edges so you can launder the runners.

223 screen play For this large folding screen, which could easily hang as three separate panels on a wall, stencil a dramatic oversize paisley design on inexpensive bifold doors from a home center. Prepare the doors with primer and add a coat of background paint; apply the pattern, borrowing colors from your fabric samples.

224 dressed for dinner Embellish purchased or ready-made slipcovers with a fabric or ribbon band at the bottom and covered-button details down the back. To make your own custom covers, check out pattern books at your local fabrics store—most companies will have a simple slipcover pattern in their home-decorating chapters.

one-hour accents

This stylish bedroom is filled with beautiful textiles, striking stencil designs, and on-trend shades of purple. You can create each accessory in an hour or less.

225 sleeping beauty For a headboard that's as pretty as it is easy, start with a piece of preprimed artist's canvas that's about 6 inches narrower than your mattress. Lay the canvas flat on a protected surface, and with a large, wide paintbrush and acrylic crafts paint, apply a background color. For a mottled effect, pick up a second color on the brush and blend it into the background while it's wet. Using small sponge rollers and acrylic paints, apply a stencil design. Once it dries, center and hang the canvas over your bed with upholstery tacks.

226 the final touch

Update a lamp to coordinate with a redecorated room. Using a soft cloth, wipe a coat of silver paint inside the lampshade and on the metal frame and harp. Buff it with a clean cloth when dry. Paint the outside and top with a finial fashioned from a drawer pull.

227 elegant bolster

Brocade satin needs little more than a single seam to transform it into a beautiful bolster pillow. Lay brocade fabric facedown over a pillow. Then lay solid-color satin lining facedown over it. Pin the two snugly together. Remove the pillow and stitch along the pinned seam. Turn right side out, insert the pillow, and tie the ends with satin ribbon.

228 tiered table

Three serving trays and a trip to the hardware store can net you a sleek bedside table. All-thread rods, secured with washers, nuts, and caps, hold up the trays, while brass caps form the feet.

229 quick triptych

Make a bedside gallery in minutes with three canvases and one stunning stencil. Paint the backgrounds the same color, and then apply the design using a foam stencil roller and three complementary shades of acrylic paint. Hang your artwork with double-faced satin ribbon.

230 chunky stands

These candleholders started as kitchen tableware. Purchase soup and salad bowls in your desired color, and epoxy them together to make shapely stands in a size you want.

fresh outlook

You can create a breezy, comfortable space on a budget. Here's how it's done.

231

232

231 unifying furniture Scour flea markets and garage sales for furniture high in function but low in cosmetic appeal. With a fresh coat of paint to unify the pieces, such as the desk and shelving units shown here, everything goes together seamlessly.

232 repurpose solutions Claim open wall space in a home office by hanging an unused bath cabinet. Tuck papers in the cubbies and hang a lunch box stocked with supplies from one of the pegs. A three-tiered basket makes a colorful display for ribbons and bows at the gift-wrapping station.

233 attractive magnets

Transform common items such as rocks into playful magnets by hot gluing ceramic block magnets to the backs. Then, to free up desk space, use magnetic containers to organize clips, staples, and more.

234 use up wallpaper

If you have a scrap of wallpaper you simply can't bear to throw away, cover the interior of a bath cabinet. Add shallow shelves to the back of the cabinet door and paper the shelf fronts and door panel with a soothing print.

235 thrifty thinking

Before you throw out or donate old clothing, salvage the good sections to embellish an accent pillow. Use fusible web to attach small pieces to a larger fabric background and create interesting designs such as this patchwork-style flower.

236 can-can

Recycle soup cans by covering the sides with pretty scrapbooking papers. Install pan-head screws through the backs of the cans and then mount the cans to a wall.

237 hand-me-downs

Brighten a piece of hand-me-down furniture with a coat of paint in a modern hue. We redid this dresser in a perky shade of green and added a changing pad for a baby's room.

238 frame fun

Why let pretty plates stay hidden in the cupboard? We elevated melamine dishes to art by hanging them on the wall and mounting empty picture frames around them for striking impact.

239 lampshade spruce-up

Enhance a neutral shade with colorful ribbons and a pretty scalloped border salvaged from a vintage handkerchief. Just glue the pieces to the shade rim, overlapping the edges and the cut ends.

For more project details, see "Dig In" on page 118.

outdoor style

Use everyday items to bring color and style to outdoor spaces. And better yet, do it on a budget.

240 bring the indoors outside Summer evenings are ideal for entertaining in the garden. Create a cozy outdoor room by skipping the standard picnic table in favor of a long wooden version spray-painted to look like stainless steel. Make sure the paint you use will withstand the elements.

241 think outside the window Bring unexpected items home to use in your garden. For example, these two plastic baskets, purchased for $1 each, serve as unexpected window boxes.

242 play with materials Frosted spray paint transforms clear glass containers. Hanging votives from a wire swag adds surprise to a garden. To get this look, spray multiple light coatings of paint on the exterior of the glass votives; twist wire around the rims to hang them.

243 paint it modern Vintage metal lawn chairs coated in metallic paint and topped with cushions are perfect for a front porch. Be sure to prep with a primer made for metal.

244 color match Sisal rugs make great porch companions (as long as you keep them out of the rain). Embellish them with acrylic exterior paints that match your color scheme. Bold stripes call attention to the rug on this porch.

245 flip for the unexpected A series of frames above a metal garden bench showcase dried leaves and flowers. The three-dimensional botanicals can be replaced each season. Use scraps of molding to create matching frames, or paint ready-made frames in black and green.

246 go bold Paint oversize house numbers on pillows and place them on a bench by the front door. Although the pillows are fair-weather decor, they're a perfect accent for summers on the porch.

247 design for change A simple length of outdoor fabric hemmed on all sides with fabric glue and punctuated with grommets screens an intimate space.

For more project details, see "Dig In" on page 118.

dream
easy...

Start in the morning and you'll be snuggling up to your new headboard tonight. These four quick projects provide all the inspiration you need.

248 underfoot or overhead Elevate a pretty rug to center stage by draping it over your headboard. Choose a lightweight woven rug that's slightly narrower than the headboard and keep it in place with clip-on curtain rings tied together with twill tape or ribbon.

249 bring the outside in
Purchased exterior shutters hang together
to make a simple headboard. Buy painted
shutters to eliminate any preparation and
simply screw them to the wall. It takes only
minutes to make this bed.

250 old looks new Paint
and fabric work wonders on this discarded
headboard. Simply select any headboard with
a paintable frame and recessed partitions you
can cover in fabric. Paint the frame and let dry.
Staple the fabric in place; cover the staples
with glued-on trim.

251 hang it today Transform a
blank canvas into over-the-bed art. Stretch
batting across the canvas front and staple
it to the back of the frame. Repeat with a
colorful patterned fabric. You need only about
a yard, so splurge on one you really like.

For more project details,
see "Dig In" on page 118.

puzzle solved!

Stumped on how to brighten a room filled with dark furniture? Let a favorite pastime inspire you.

252 cool complements Icy blues and metallic silver accents make comfortable companions to the dark brown of the leather sectional in this family room. Pulling in lighter shades of brown for the rug and throw pillows adds a third layer of color to the room.

253 domino effect Dig into your game stash to get the pieces you'll need for this art project. Take a few dominoes to the copy shop and play with different sizes and arrangements on a color photocopier, laying the pieces facedown directly on the glass. Finish your artwork with silver metallic frames.

254 snack attack Satisfy hungry family and guests by keeping these paper-cone popcorn holders on hand. Cut out a circle from brown card stock using scallop-edge decorative scissors and shape it into a cone. Thread ribbon and a punched paper circle around the cone. Add a parchment-paper lining to prevent seepage.

255 toss across Add a playful addition to a plain linen throw pillow using the numbered squares of a crossword puzzle. Take the puzzle to a copy shop, photocopy it onto fabric, and sew the panel to the pillow. If desired, pen family names or other sayings onto the crossword for added fun.

256 a no-sew throw There's no need to spend a lot of time and money searching for the perfect throw. Buy an inexpensive blanket and embellish it with iron-on patches and ribbon with self-binding tape.

257 time to shine When you want to brighten a wall in a unique way, metallic leafing will do the trick. The silver leaf comes in sheets and is easy to apply over leafing adhesive. Use a brush to burnish the sheets onto the tacky surface for a seamless finish.

258 fit to be accessorized Reinforce the fun-loving nature of your family's rec room with dominoes, dice, and game tiles displayed inside glass canisters on the mantel.

259 easy as 1,2,3 Keeping score never looked this good. Give a standard notepad a face-lift with a cover-up cut from decorative paper. Then add a scalloped medallion using a large punch and finish it off with a rubber-stamped, embossed initial in the center.

260 card tricks Choose cards that will reinforce your color scheme and decoupage them onto a plain white tray. Place some faceup and some facedown, overlapping as desired. Adhere them with decoupage medium, and seal the surface to protect the cards.

For more project details, see "Dig In" on page 118.

ready, set, paint!

A can of spray paint has transformative powers. Check out the products and techniques we used to create these fun and surprisingly easy accents.

261 blackboard beauty

Paint plastic frames using no-prep spray paint designed for use on plastic. Spray the backing with chalkboard paint and reassemble.

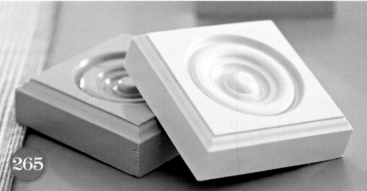

262 spray-on mirror Mirror-finish spray paint and a tree silhouette add vintage charm to an old window. Freehand a design on the back of the window and add mirror finish in several light coats. Or use a stencil to add a different motif to the front of the pane before spraying the mirror finish on the back of the glass.

263 great redo Spray paint always makes for a smooth finish on large pieces of furniture, such as this cabinet. When the paint dries, coat the surface with polyurethane to add sheen.

264 crafty place setting Chair backs coated with chalkboard paint provide erasable name "cards." To take the theme even further, use paint on a tray to create a menu board.

265 corner coasters Leftover spray paint is perfect for making these coasters. Purchase corner blocks in the molding section of a home center and set the pieces on small cans for spraying. For durability, spray the painted blocks with polyurethane.

266 chandelier update Black paint adds instant style to the glass shades of this metal chandelier. Use an adhesive-backed stencil and paint designed for glass. Cover the shades to protect them from overspray.

267 color a table Unfinished wood is the perfect canvas for paint. Sand the surface lightly, remove the sanding dust with a tack cloth, and then spray the piece with one thin coat of primer and several thin coats of paint, allowing each coat to dry before adding the next. Protect the painted surface with two coats of polyurethane.

For more project details, see "Dig In" on page 118.

added attractions

Perk up a dining room with a spring-fresh palette of robin's-egg blue, cocoa, and tangerine. Spread the hues with these nine colorful ideas.

268

269

270

271

268 background beauty

The easiest and cheapest way to launch a new color scheme is to paint the walls. Be adventurous—paint is easy to change whenever a new hue catches your eye.

269 painted lampshades

Fabric lampshades dress up this dated chandelier for less than $10. To make your own, coat purchased fabric shades with two layers of gesso so paint won't bleed through. Paint a pattern in two shades of blue and add dots of taupe, white, and blue using the rounded end of an artist's paintbrush.

270 chip off the block
Shop for accessories armed with paint chips that match your palette.

271 ribbon-wrapped table
Add personality to a boring piece of furniture with patterned ribbon. Wrap the ribbon around the apron of a table and hold in place with double-sided tape.

272 mix-and-match dinnerware
Stretch your budget and still get something fresh. Opt for new special-occasion patterned salad plates to pair with your everyday dinnerware. Choose complementary hues, such as orange with blue or lavender with spring green.

273 clip-and-go curtains

Combine off-the-bolt fabric with simple no-sew techniques to create these easy curtains. Press under the top and bottom edges of the fabric, and fuse. Attach curtain clips to the top, and slide them on the curtain rod.

274 papered cabinet

Cover the back of a cabinet with wrapping paper in a subtle pattern and color. At less than $5 a roll, wrapping paper is a budget-friendly option. To make this a temporary treatment, spray the back of the paper with fugitive adhesive or use clear plastic tacks.

275 color-coded
Support the room's color scheme by showcasing a collection in an open cabinet. Prized possessions can add the season's favorite hues—here, tangerine and aqua.

276 button up
A ready-made seat cushion looks custom-made, thanks to covered buttons stitched on top. Stretch ribbon around the buttons to make an "X" and tack the ribbon at each end.

For more project details, see "Dig In" on page 118.

277 hollywood glitz
Transform your clear glass vases with shiny paint. Wash them in hot soapy water, rinse well, and let dry thoroughly. Use adhesive-backed paper or painter's tape to mask off a design. Apply a metallic paint formulated for glass (we used chrome spray). When it's dry, carefully remove the paper or tape.

mix up the
metallics

The hottest trend in home decor, metallic finishes can be found in spray cans, on wallpaper and fabric, and in pens, paints, and stamp pads.

278 purple passion For a conversation piece, paint a chair a sensual shade of aubergine and cover the seat with metallic patterned fabric. We chose an oversize damask. Look for orphan chairs at antiques shops and garage sales. When there's just one, you can often snag a bargain.

279 silver sidekick Transform a small table into a high-style accent with hammered-silver spray paint. Start with a coat of gray primer and then add one or two coats of silver. The look is as impressive as an expensive mirrored table but at a fraction of the cost.

280 luxury lighting Add beautiful metallic color to a drum shade with satin ribbon. Vary the widths for interest, securing the bands with double-stick tape. (Glue will bleed through the ribbon.) Add luster to the inside of the shade by rubbing on gold metallic paste, using a soft cloth to apply it.

281 tailored jackets Feel free to judge these books by their covers. Exquisite handmade papers make journals more than a good read. Remove the existing jackets and use them for your patterns. Cut the paper to size and then replace the original jacket with the new cover for an elegant display. Create computer-generated title labels if you like, and adhere them to the spines.

Elegant handmade papers with metallic designs add **sophistication** to your **creative projects**.

282 artistic tiles While you're embellishing home furnishings with metallics, reserve some of the leftover product to make artful tiles. Cut lumber into 7½×8-inch pieces. Apply metallic faux finishes to some blocks, and cover others with wallpaper.

283 hardware update Don't toss out your drapery rods and finials every time you redecorate. Quickly transform them with metallics. We covered one with gold cording, a second with copper leaf, and a third with rub-on color.

284 beautiful boxes For storage or for gifting, cover boxes of all sizes with wallpaper scraps. You might even want to keep boxes originally intended as gifts to add a touch of glamour to almost any room. Use decoupage medium or the strongest wallpaper adhesive available to mount the papers to the boxes.

285 gold rush Strike it rich with this easy centerpiece, crafted from a discount-store basket and quarry rock. Medium-size river stones coated with silver, gold, and copper leaf look fabulous in a wire bowl sprayed with bronze metallic paint. Our favorite rocks are those that allow portions of the stone to show through.

286 fit for a queen One lone chair spotted at an antiques shop for $40 gets a new look with bronze spray paint and metallic-thread fabric. To jazz up your own chair, remove the seat and lightly sand any rough spots. Apply a coat of gray primer, followed by two coats of a metallic color. Cover the seat with fabric using a staple gun, and you have accent seating that will mix with the finest furnishings.

For more project details, see "Dig In" on page 118.

287

288

citrus punch!

Fashion a work space that's sure to keep you energized with its palette of juicy hues and creative storage solutions.

289

PEACE LIKE A RIVER LEIF ENGER

emotional ROOMS

THE HOME ORGANIZING WORKBOOK

pillows & throws

287 window dressing For these panels, cut fabric to fit the window, adding ½-inch seam allowances and allowing for a 4-inch band of coordinating fabric at the bottom and inside of each panel. Cut 4-inch bands for the bottom and one side of each panel, adding ½-inch seam allowances. Sew piping from another coordinating fabric. Sew the pieces together, placing the piping between the panels and bands. Hang from a curtain rod using ring clips. For the shade, cut fabric to fit the window, adding ½-inch seam allowances on the bottom and sides and 2 inches at the top. Hem the bottom and side edges and staple the top edge to the back of a 1×2 board cut to fit inside the window. Around the board, wrap two lengths of ribbon, each twice as long as the fabric, and attach the board to the top of the window. Use the ribbon ties to adjust the shade.

288 flower power Update a purchased lampshade in minutes using scrapbooking embellishments. To attach these fabric flowers, we poked color-coordinated brads into the flower centers and through the paper shade, securing them on the inside.

289 give 'em the slip Extend the life of old chairs with custom covers. Measure the chair and cut your fabric, overcutting each piece by about 3 inches to allow for pin-fitting. Lay the pieces on the chair, right sides down. Pin them together inside out, following the contours of the chair; carefully remove. Stitch all seams, turn right side out, and place on the chair. Pin the bottom for a hem, stitch, and press.

290 two's company Finding a hutch to fit a small space and an even smaller budget isn't always easy. Solve the problem by stacking a bookcase atop a dresser. To make them appear as one, prime and paint the unfinished pieces the same color. For added punch, paint the back of the bookcase blue and then use spray adhesive to attach decorative papers to the dresser's drawer fronts.

291 picture perfect A vintage metal roasting pot turns into a clever photo holder when labeled with letter magnets. Photos stay out of sight but still within easy reach.

292 mix and match Turn mismatched thrift-shop frames into a pretty display by painting them all white. Frames without glass are usually less expensive; and are great for displaying decorative paper cut to fit the openings. Let the paper be the star or top it with a wooden letter, a photo, or any object you love.

293 top dog Give your pooch a snazzy spot to rest with an easy-sew bed. To successfully mix bold patterns, stick to colors of the same intensity.

294 smart storage Complementary storage containers tuck away clutter and add a pop of color above a neutral desk. A variety of shapes and sizes guarantees everything fits.

297 for the birds

Make a big statement with wall decals, like these caged birds. Follow the manufacturer's instructions for applying the decals; use a level to keep them straight.

295 stripe it rich

Make a mock rug from a canvas drop cloth. Spread the cloth tightly across two sheets of 4×8 plywood, stapling it to the backs. Roll on two coats of primer; let dry. Measure and mark stripes. Use painter's tape to mask off every other stripe and then paint; let dry. Repeat for the remaining stripes. Apply two coats of finish sealer. Remove the cloth from the plywood, turn it over, and hem the edges with double-sided carpet tape.

296 skirt the issue

Lend feminine flair to a rolling desk chair by painting the back pink and adding a frilly seat cover.

For more project details, see "Dig In" on page 118.

pages
66–69 Cottage Retreat

Fork It Over

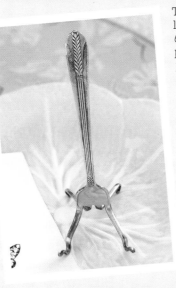

To craft a clever easel like the one on *page 68,* use needle-nose pliers to pull the outer prongs of a fork forward and the center prongs backward until the fork can stand on its own. Use the pliers to bend the ends of the front prongs up so they can hold artwork, business cards, or recipes. Curl the ends of the back prongs into spirals for a decorative touch. To keep the pliers from scratching the finish, place a cloth between the pliers and the prongs. For a grouping of artwork, make easels in different sizes by mixing dinner and salad forks.

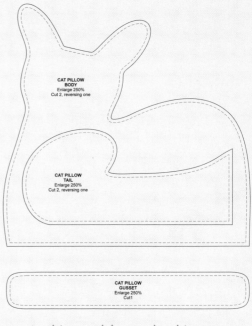

CAT PILLOW
BODY
Enlarge 250%
Cut 2, reversing one

CAT PILLOW
TAIL
Enlarge 250%
Cut 2, reversing one

CAT PILLOW
GUSSET
Enlarge 250%
Cut 1

Scale the pattern to the size you desire!

pages
70–73 Amazing As Is

Sweet light

Imagine this wire-fence chandelier at your next garden-inspired party.

Grab:
Wire fence, lampshade frame, decorative chain, threaded lamp nipple, electrical compression splices, annealed wire, light socket, cord with plug, glass lampshade, glass garland, Chinese lantern lightbulbs, metal-color spray paint, fishing line, heavy-duty wire cutters, heavy-duty pliers, metal file, screwdriver.

Go:
1. Disassemble the lampshade; the only component needed is the top section with the center piece and crossbars.
2. Gather all of the metal items, except the fence, and spray-paint them so they match the fencing.
3. Measure and cut the fence so it fits around the lampshade frame. Then join the cut ends of the fence together with electrical compression splices, and wire the lampshade frame to the fence. Using heavy-duty pliers, turn under the cut ends of the fence around the bottom of the shade to hang the garland.
4. Wire the lamp, add the glass lampshade, and attach the chain to hang the lamp.
5. Make wire hangers for the Chinese lantern lightbulbs and hang them from the fence with fishing line. Add the garland.

upclose

pages
74–75 Sleep on It

No-Nonsense Nailheads

For evenly spaced nailheads without the hassle of trying to align each one by hand, try using nailhead trim by the roll. Each nail is attached to an easy-to-use flexible tack strip, ensuring a professional look every time. Or use a tool such as a Quick Nailer, which allows you to accurately set up to five nails at a time—and keeps your fingers safely out of the way.

Nailhead trim adds a classic finish to furniture.

upclose

Glass with class

Shop flea markets and antiques malls for glassware you can transform into functional items such as candleholders to set on a nightstand or pretty catchalls for loose change on the dresser. Less-than-perfect items work especially well for this purpose and are very affordable. Candlewick glass, *left,* is popular and readily found, and it's available in hundreds of interesting shapes and many colors, such as pink, blue, green, and caramel.

pages
80–81 Beachy Keen

The perfect vintage

Vintage fabrics are much beloved for their old-fashioned colors and patterns, but be choosy when buying them. Here are some tips when shopping:

Do a little research. Check eBay or a local antiques mall to find out the going rates for tablecloths, napkins, and other textiles, both in "pristine" and "as is" condition.

Give fabric a once-over. Look for obvious stains, then hold an item up to the light to reveal threadbare spots and grease splotches. These areas might make a vintage piece unusable, or you might decide to feature only a small portion of a stained item—as a pillow or in a frame, for instance.

To frame a swatch of vintage fabric (as on *page 80*), determine what portion of the fabric should show through the frame. Use the frame's hardboard backer as a template to cut the fabric to size. Stiffen the fabric so it's easier to work with by spraying it with starch and pressing with an iron or by adhering fusible interfacing to the wrong side, then slip it into the frame. Instant wall art!

pages
82–83 Budget Beauty

Buttoned Up

A button-tufted upholstered headboard brings elegance to the bedroom. While it's virtually impossible to buy a new one for less than $100, you can make one for much less from medium-density fiberboard (MDF).

Cut a piece of MDF to fit behind your bed (you may need to join two pieces). Hot-glue cushion foam to the front of the headboard, leaving an overhang just wide enough to wrap around the edges but not around to the back.

Lay the covered MDF facedown atop upholstery fabric. Wrap the excess fabric around to the back, pulling the foam over the edges in the process, and staple the fabric to the back of the MDF. It's easiest to stretch and staple the center of each side first and then secure the rest of the fabric.

Measure and mark where the buttons will go on the back of the MDF. At each mark, drill a hole through the back and out the front of the fabric (drill slowly to avoid ripping the fabric). To tuft, thread wire through a covered button and then push the wire through each hole. Pull the wire taut so the button indents the foam and then twist in place on the back of the MDF.

upclose

pages
84–87 Better Than Ever

Large-scale stencils

A stenciled pattern breathes life into a dull room. Begin with clean walls. If they're freshly painted, wait several days. Mark with a pencil around the room where the pattern should go, using a level.

upclose

Apply spray adhesive to the back of the template and adhere the template to the wall at the starting point. Using a stencil brush, apply stencil cream or wall paint in a dabbing motion. To prevent paint from seeping under the template, apply in multiple thin coats.

For more depth, dab a second color, applying it lightly. When you've painted the entire template, peel it off the wall, wipe any paint smears off the back, then reapply to the next portion of the wall. Repeat until the design is finished, then let dry.

Silhouette Pillow Appliqués

Follow these instructions for the perfect pillow:

Cut a circle of kraft paper slightly larger than the desired silhouette size. Cut one circle from fabric. Fold the circle in half and use it to cut two half-circles from a second fabric, adding a ½-inch seam allowance to the straight edge for the center back seam. Cut a ¾-inch-wide side strip from the second fabric 2 inches longer than is needed to fit around the perimeter of the pillow.

Take a digital photo of your child's profile. Use a computer to size the photo; print. Copy the outline onto tracing paper. Transfer onto fusible web; cut out. Fuse the shape onto felt. Cut out the felt shape just beyond the edges. Remove the paper backing and position the felt shape, web side down, on the pillow front. Fuse in place.

Press under 1 inch at one end of the side strip. Beginning with the pressed end, pin the side strip to the pillow front with right sides together; the opposite end will lap under the pressed end. Use a ½-inch seam allowance to sew the side strip to the pillow front. Clip the seam allowances. Sew the pillow backs together at the center, leaving an 8-inch opening. Sew the opposite edge of the side strip to the pillow back. Clip the seam allowances. Turn right side out. Insert a pillow form or stuffing and slip-stitch the opening closed.

pages
88–89 Light and Bright

DIY design Finding a perfectly coordinated stencil for a decorating project isn't always easy, particularly when you want something oversize. Instead of settling for one you don't love, make your own in three simple steps:

1. Enlarge clip art or a pattern from the room to the correct size on a photocopier (for supersize designs, have a copy shop print it for you).

2. Trace the design onto a large sheet of template plastic, available in the quilting section of fabrics stores. (Thinner plastic requires a careful touch when cutting, and cardboard isn't waterproof or pliable.)

3. Place the plastic over a cutting board and then cut out the design with a crafts knife, leaving at least 1 inch of solid plastic around the motif.

pages
90–93 Vintage Beauty

Finding Fantastic Fibers

Start shopping for vintage textiles at these stops.
Shows:
• Brimfield May's Antique Market, Inc., Brimfield, MA; maysbrimfield.com.
• First Monday Trade Days, Canton, TX; firstmondaycanton.com.
• Marburger Farm Antique Show, Round Top, TX; roundtop-marburger.com.
• Rose Bowl Flea Market, Pasadena, CA; rgcshows.com.

Online:
• eBay.com. Huge inventory in a wide variety.
• dewittco.com. Good source for vintage advertising feed sacks.
• thevintagetable.net. Large selection of vintage tablecloths from the '40s and '50s.

upclose

Beyond the chair
Simple chair legs make perfect holders for hand towels. Cut the side runners down to 3 inches and install by drilling from the inside of a cabinet into the runners. Or screw blocks of wood to the runners and screw through the blocks into a wall or cabinet.

Cut it! This embossed panel is not what it seems. It's actually plastic designed to look like tin. Cut it with a utility knife to fit a backsplash or a refrigerator front. It's impact- and stain-resistant and is suitable for wet spaces. Check it out (item #240793) at **lowes.com**.

pages
98–99 Fresh Outlook

Paper panache Customize a plain clipboard and small empty buckets with a decoupaged layer of patterned papers. For a durable finish, use a decoupage adhesive to adhere and seal the paper. Here's how to do it:

1. Brush decoupage adhesive onto the back of the patterned paper and smooth the paper onto the clipboard or the bucket sides. Let dry.
2. Brush a second coat of decoupage adhesive onto the paper; let dry.
3. For extra durability, brush a third coat of decoupage adhesive onto the paper; let dry thoroughly.

pages
100–101 Outdoor Style

Double-duty awning This simple canopy features fabric suspended above sapling supports. Grommets along the fabric's edges keep it in place.

✳ **Look for similar awning supplies at pier1.com, target.com, and worldmarket.com.**

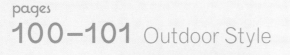

Best Places to Find Vintage Treasures

1. Beaver Creek Antiques Market in Hagerstown, MD; **beavercreekantiques.com.** "Great stuff in small booths."

2. D.C. Big Flea in Chantilly, VA; **damorepromotions.com.** "It's more flea market than antiques show."

3. Old Glory Antique Marketplace in Frederick, MD; **oldgloryantiques.com.** "Shoppers always find something there."

4. New Oxford Antique Center in New Oxford, PA; **newoxfordantiquecenter.com.** "The variety is super."

pages
102–103 Dream Easy

Headboard Smarts

For a smooth finish when covering an artist's canvas with fabric, start by stapling in the center of each side, pulling the fabric tight before attaching it. Work back and forth across the canvas to create a tight fit without distorting the fabric pattern. Fabric with some stretch will give you the best fit. Take note: Stretching a geometric pattern is difficult.

Clever reuse!

Think beyond the rod to turn clip-on curtain rings into handy anchors for a headboard slipcover. Use metal rings for a more contemporary look and wooden rings for a cottage feel.

upclose

A quick wrap

Painted shutters stand in for a headboard in this colorful room. A bold-print bolster pillow and easy artwork finish the bright design.

pages
104–105 Puzzle Solved

Make it metallic

Leafing products have become more user-friendly. Look for leafing in packages of sheets. Brush leafing adhesive onto the surface and separate the leafing sheet from its paper backing. Gently lay the leafing onto the adhesive and use a brush to burnish it onto the surface. If you miss a spot, just burnish a leftover fleck in place. Today's products result in a seamless finish as you leaf adjoining squares and fill in spots.

Snack time

To assemble the popcorn cone, layer a 9-inch parchment-paper circle and a 10-inch brown card-stock circle as shown, and roll them into a cone. Thread ribbon through a 3-inch punched circle and tie it around the cone.

Use scalloped-edge scissors to add a decorative finish to paper circles.

pages
106–107
Ready, Set, Paint

An expert tip…
Use spray primer if the project starts with raw wood. Look for a combination primer/paint to eliminate this step when spraying metal.

Spray Style

Hyacinth
Tanzanite
Ocean Breeze
Celery
Lime
Aquamarine
Blue Hyacinth
Bonnet Blue
Hammered Black

Unlike standard paints, spray paint is available in limited colors. Start by first choosing a hue. There are a variety of fun finishes, including blackboard, mirror, and metallic. There also are products designed for use on plastic, metal, wood, glass, and more.

Silhouette Stencils

A tree design was painted freehand on this dramatic mirror. If you're less certain about your painting skills, create a stencil.

1. Print an illustration.
2. Use a photocopier to enlarge the design to the desired size and adhere it to cardboard with spray adhesive.
3. Use a crafts knife to cut away the design, leaving behind the outline.
4. To use the stencil, place it on the mirror using repositionable spray adhesive. Apply paint inside the outline using a pouncing motion.

pages
108–109 Added Attractions

upclose

Customize a Vinyl Roller Shade

1. Apply painter's tape to create white stripes.
2. Paint the shade using a foam roller and latex paint. Let dry.
3. For a soft finish, thin paint 1:1 with acrylic matte medium and lightly brush the mixture on the shade to mimic woven fabric. Let dry. Remove the tape.
4. Glue ball fringe to the shade edge.

110–113 Mix Up the Metallics

Artistic tiles

What you need:
- 8-inch-wide clear pine
- Metallic finishes
- Stamps and stencils
- Metallic wallpapers
- Brushes, sandpaper

Make it:
Cut the boards into 8-inch sections and sand all edges smooth. If you don't have your own power saw, ask a home center to make the cuts.

(Left to right from top left)
Tile 1: Paint all surfaces, including the back, with dark chocolate-color paint; let dry. Stamp the design using copper color ink.
Tiles 2, 4, 6, 8, 10, and 12: Cover alternating tiles with metallic-finish wallpaper. Plan the placement of your pattern and then cut the paper larger all around. Coat the paper with wallpaper paste. Fold up the sides first and wrap the strips around the corners. Then fold in the top and bottom. Smooth out any bubbles. Quickly wipe off any wallpaper paste that seeps onto the paper surface. Cover the back with a paper square cut slightly smaller than the board. **Note:** If you don't finish the board backs, your wood may warp.
Tile 3: Paint the entire board with black acrylic paint; let dry. Coat the front and sides with leaf sizing, following manufacturer's instructions. Cut copper leaf into squares that measure ¼ the size of the board top. Apply the leaf, allowing some of the background to show through. Spray with sealer. Let it dry.

Tile 5: Paint the entire board with dark chocolate-color paint; let dry. Lightly mist the board with bronze spray. Stencil a design in the middle.
Tile 7: Follow the instructions for Tile 3 but substitute gold leaf for the copper leaf.
Tile 9: Paint the entire board with dark chocolate-color paint. Using a fine tip pen in gold, loosely scribble something that resembles words across the board.
Tile 11: Follow the instructions for Tile 3 and apply gold, silver, and copper leaf randomly.

114–117 Citrus Punch

Stitch a slipcover

Give a desk chair style by sewing a skirt for it. Measure seat from front to back, starting and stopping at bottom edge. Repeat side to side. Add 2 inches all around and cut from muslin. Center muslin over seat and trace along bottom edge. Make slits in muslin around chair-back spindles. Pleat fabric at front corners. Trim pattern, allowing ½-inch seam allowance. Allow extra length at center back between spindles to equal length of ruffle skirting. Mark pleat at front corners. Cut out main fabric. Cut bias strips of main fabric and cover piping cord. Fuse interfacing to wrong side of main fabric. Pleat corners. Stitch piping cord around outside edge, clipping piping cord at corners. Determine length of ruffle drop plus seam allowance. Cut bias strips of contrasting fabric. Hem and gather ruffle. Stitch ruffle to seat.

upclose

Custom canine comfort

Stitching a dog bed is a great way to pamper your pet. Here's how:

- Cut two circles of washable fabric 31 inches in diameter, which includes seam allowances; set aside.

- Cut 4-inch strips of the same fabric for the gusset, piecing them short end to short end to equal the circumference of the circles.

- With right sides together, pin one long edge of the gusset to one circle and stitch together. Repeat with the other circle and the other long edge of the gusset, being sure to leave an opening for stuffing.

- Turn the cover right side out, and trim and press the seams. Stuff, then whipstitch the opening closed.

upclose

organize

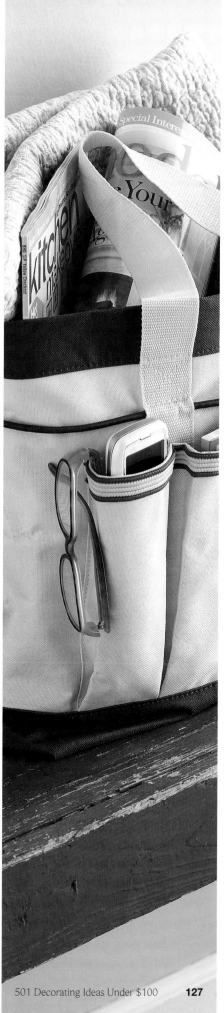

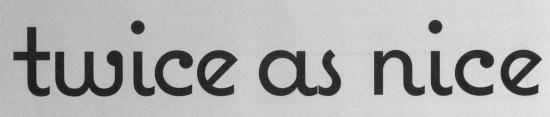

twice as nice

These storage pieces can pull double duty if they're strategically placed and outfitted with a little bling.

entryway

299 treat time Stash treats for Pooch on the desktop.

299

301 singing in the rain Stand umbrellas in a cylindrical vase in lieu of a flower arrangement.

300

301

298 stellar substitute Transform a dish-drying rack into a shoe tree.

298

300 off the hook Shop around for cute hooks to hold purses, leashes, and book bags.

If you don't already have **an old desk** languishing in the attic, find an **inexpensive** one at a thrift store.

302 hang time Hang a finished piece as artwork and for inspiration.

303 hook, line, and sinker Coat hooks hold cutting tools—a clever break from the usual basket storage.

304 on display Fabrics stay in sight with clear-front boxes.

305 clever storage Boost storage by adding a small hutch to house supplies.

sewing room

closet

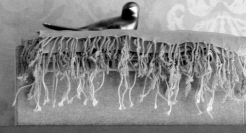

306 toilet paper tricks Mount tissue holders under shelves to hang bags.

307 on display Keep earrings in pairs on framed Aida cloth.

308 what a dish Toss everyday jewelry and pocket change into a pretty dish, such as this deviled-egg plate.

309 hung up Clip scarves and hats neatly in place with fishing wire and clothespins.

310 lunch time Leather lunch boxes add shots of color.

311 at the end Bean-filled stuffed animals make cute bookends.

kid's room

312 magnet masterpieces An added magnetic strip accommodates refrigerator-art runover.

313 tidy up Small organizers—miniature buckets on a lazy Susan and wicker baskets—make for quick and easy cleanup.

314 on a roll Use the underside of a shelf for more storage; here, paper-towel bars hold kraft paper. (Clip on a couple of clothespins to keep it from curling.)

Use shelves to **maximize vertical space** in the closet. Hung low in a kid's room, **wee ones** can reach for or put away supplies independently.

Coat basic bookcases in an **earthy neutral brown** for versatility. Then convert them into a **work space** or pair side-by-side for a **buffet**.

office

315 table topper Top bookshelves with a slab door for an instant desk.

316 lined up Shelf liner brightens up the dark recesses of a basic bookcase.

317 silverware storage
A silverware tray and bright bins organize work stuff without looking stuffy.

318 down the drain Turn an unused dish drainer into a holder for files.

dining room

319 two of a kind Place two bookshelves side-by-side for a long expanse of storage space.

319

320 roll it up Store napkins in a utensil caddy.

320

321 stair steps Maximize vertical space by placing small items on a tiered shelf designed for a pantry.

321

322 from the kitchen Stash spare linens in a pretty baking dish.

322

Bon Appetit!

For more project details, see "Dig In" on page 174.

double duty

Three hardworking storage units
get you doubly organized.

art desk

party cart

323 second use Turn a rolling cart into an art station. With a durable work surface on top and both open and concealed cubbies below, you'll feel truly creative when you sit here.

324 added space Use the drop side panel as an extra work surface. Pull up a simple stool and you have an impromptu desk for on-the-spot artwork.

325 for inspiration Tack swatches and sketches to the inside of the door. They'll inspire you while adding style and color to your work area.

326 party time Convert a kitchen cart into party central. Because it rolls, the cart can go wherever the fun is happening.

327 hooked Keep snack and drink recipes handy in folders on the inside of the door. Forget how to mix your best friend's drink? You've got the answer within easy reach.

328

kitchen

329

guest room

328 baker's solution Control kitchen clutter with the help of added storage. Convert an armoire into a baker's corner by stacking bowls on the shelves and storing measuring cups and spoons in the drawers.

329 out-of-town help Help your guests feel at home by filling an armoire with all the usual home amenities: towels, shampoo, conditioner, toothbrush, and more.

A tall and skinny armoire with **ample drawer space and three display shelves** fits into even the tiniest room.

330

bathroom

330 storage smarts

Use an inexpensive shelving unit as an étagère and keep bath supplies in orderly cubbies. Baskets and storage bins keep the shelves looking tidy.

entryway

331 easy reach Add hooks above the bench to hang your essentials. Not only are your duds readily available, they make a graphic wall display.

332 playful pillows Top the bench with decorative pillows. Rather than playing it safe with dull matching fabrics, go with a theme for an inviting variety.

333 for fido Keep pet dishes out of sight by tucking them inside a cubby. A place mat underneath offers a jolt of color and protects the bench from spills.

For more project details, see "Dig In" on page 174.

this & that...

Put clutter in its place by rethinking how furniture can adapt to your needs—now and in the future.

mudroom

334 at the door With a place for everything—mail, dog treats, picnic supplies, and toys—this storage unit encourages mudroom organization.

335 in the sun A sunroom is for lounging and enjoying a good book. Make it easier to relax by keeping the essentials neatly organized in a storage unit. Books, pillows, and decorations all have a home here.

336 eye pleasing Back the shelves with wallpaper to add pattern and distinguish the shelf from the wall.

sunroom

crafts room

337 crafty creation
A shallow hanging cupboard provides plenty of storage for small items, such as ribbon, paint, beads, and stamps.

338 wrapped up
Add finials to the top to corral wrapping paper, while keeping it easy to grab.

339 bow tied Thread spools of ribbon onto a tension rod.

340 second use | A low-cost cupboard provides the right amount of put-away space in most any kitchen. Stack bowls, label containers, and display vintage towels for added orderliness.

back porch

Herb Gardener

341

342

343

341 in the garden In a protected outdoor space, a metal baker's rack holds all your gardening gear.

342 tool time Garden tools make pretty displays—and stay neatly organized— when hung from S hooks.

343 read the signs Showcase a vintage sign on a couple of S hooks. Score a sign at your favorite flea market, or search online for a wide variety of vintage tin and metal decor.

344 bath time Turn your bathroom into a relaxing retreat by showcasing pretty towels, hanging scrubbers and a robe from S hooks, and displaying lotions and perfumes.

For more project details, see "Dig In" on page 174.

triple play

With just a few simple and inexpensive changes, a stock bookcase takes on three distinct personalities.

before

This unfinished piece desperately needed a dose of character.

new country

345 for love of country To create a soft country look, prime and paint the bookcase cream.

346 sophisticated wallpaper Glue wallpaper in a soft eggshell-and-floral pattern to the back of each opening for unexpected and pretty detail.

347 behind the curtain Hang linen café curtains on a tension rod for concealed storage in the lower third.

sleek modern

348 rich character Create a contemporary look by covering the entire bookcase with ebony gel stain, which is easy to apply and adds deep color.

349 roll down Buy a light-color linen roller shade to fit the width and height of the bookcase. Install it at the top to hide clutter. Add a pretty pull to distinguish the shade.

350 boxy organization Fill the shelves with boxes and files in neutral tones. You'll keep clutter from view while continuing your color palette.

classic cottage

351 ivory and ebony Prime, sand, and paint the bookcase tan for timeless appeal. Black accents complete the classic look.

352 hidden away Board-and-batten shutters with cutouts always create a traditional cottage feel. Custom-order shutters online and attach them to the front of the bookcase with cabinetry hinges.

353 bolted shut Finish the bookcase with a forged-iron shutter bolt.

For more project details, see "Dig In" on page 174.

power
powder
room

These simple solutions boost storage space and turn the bath into a spalike sanctuary.

354 on the move
Short on counter space? This patterned serving tray works as a movable vanity. Store it in a linen closet when not in use or before guests arrive.

355 in the bin If your cabinets don't have drawers, add bins to the shelves. A length of elastic stitched or glued inside will keep items in place (the same trick works for gym bags).

356 slide of hand Organize under-vanity space with side- or bottom-mount sliding racks. Fill handled pails with frequently accessed beauty supplies.

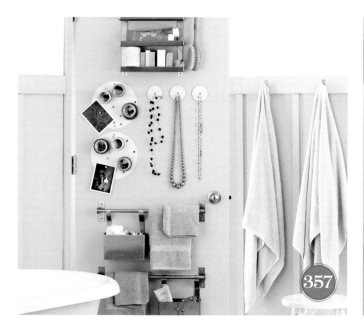

357 door of opportunity Can doors ever store! On the back of this one, two styles of spice racks hold lotions, potions, and jewelry, and brushes hang on hooks. Adhesive-backed hooks get the overflow, and kitchen storage bins corral primping products.

358 out of the kitchen When it comes to storage, if it works in the often-humid heart of the home, it will work in a bathroom, too. These wall-mounted utensil boxes are just the right size for his-and-hers grooming essentials and can easily come on and off for use in other areas of the room.

359 storage on high Inexpensive pantry shelving stocked with bins and towels does a mighty organizational job above the toilet. Label the bins to easily locate items.

Vertical space is an often-overlooked gold mine of storage opportunities. **Maximize your storage** by adding wall shelves or cabinets.

360 curb service Grab a broken chair from the curb on trash day and convert it into a bath shelf by cutting off the legs and most of the seat, then screwing a piece of trim to the top. Attach old-time faucet handles for hanging supplies and bumper pads to protect the wall from scratches. Sink screws through the trim piece into wall studs or use screw anchors.

361 small world Take control of a medicine cabinet with storage solutions that organize odd-size items. Use adhesive-backed clips to mount toothbrushes and razors to the back wall. Small freestanding shelves make the most of the tight space. Keep little items in check with pretty makeup cases, jars, and clear boxes.

kitchen
control

Keep the kitchen efficient
and user-friendly with
these organizational ideas.

362

363

364

365

362 hang it up Corral spice jars, measuring spoons, and other small kitchen utensils inside hanging storage accessories that make use of space along the sides of a kitchen island. Add labels to the spice jars for easy identification.

363 write stuff Keep track of kids' schedules and grocery lists by turning the inside of a cabinet door into a chalkboard. Screw pegboard over another panel and store small items from hooks.

364 contain yourself Get easy access to often-used ingredients by housing them inside a handy pull-out drawer. Install drawer slides on the bottom shelf of the island and paint the drawer to match.

365 sliding solution Add an undermount basket drawer beneath the island and gain slide-out storage for oven mitts, trivets, and other often-used tools. Its open design allows you to see what's inside—even from a distance.

366 rack and roll Store long, slender items such as paper-towel rolls, a rolling pin, and kitchen wrap inside a wine rack mounted underneath an island's work surface. A cutting-board holder designed for the interior of a cabinet door also works well mounted to the side of the shelf.

366

367 get a handle on it
Mount a wooden dowel between two decorative brackets underneath a cabinet and hang spoons, spatulas, whisks, and ladles from S hooks.

368 pot luck No room for a pot rack? Custom fit a pegboard on the kitchen wall and hang pots, pans, strainers, and the like from hooks. Conceal the rough-cut edges of the board with pieces of mitered trim attached to the sides.

369 curtain coverage Keep things tidy underneath a sink stand with plastic bins and a filing cabinet stocked with pantry items. Mount a simple spring-loaded rod underneath the counter and hang a short curtain to conceal the area.

370 shelf style Stop fumbling with cabinet doors and call on a closet organizer as an open shelving unit in the kitchen. Display glassware, favorite platters, and frequently used items on the adjustable, spacious shelves.

LAUNDRY
softeners

Put a happy new spin on your laundry routine with these clever storage solutions.

371 decorate with character Hanging shelves in tight quarters is a great way to maximize vertical space. The collections—vintage washboards, clothespins, and a glass soap canister—hint at the room's hardworking purpose.

372 curtain call Simple curtain panels strung on a tension rod hide a washer and dryer between laundry loads. With the curtains closed, this back entry looks as charmingly decorated as any other space in the house.

373 center of attention Paint windows a complementary color to make them the room's focal point.

374 brighten up A nook with two windows is always a pleasant spot to do laundry. But even if your laundry room lacks daylight, brighten it with yellow and white stripes painted on the walls. First paint the walls white. Use a level and pencil to mark the locations of the stripes; then mask the lines with painter's tape. Paint on yellow stripes using a 4-inch foam roller.

375 small-space solutions Make the most of an awkward corner by hanging a shelf up high and using it to store towels or other supplies. Use wire baskets, which also can hold clothespins until they're needed. To maximize space, stash an ironing board beneath the shelf and tuck a rolling cart into the alcove.

376 contain yourself Gather vintage wire baskets and covered jars to store laundry supplies within view. Keep the containers handy on the dryer top or a rolling cart. Find examples at **containerstore.com**, **ikea.com**, and **stacksandstacks.com**.

377 functional furniture A dated entertainment center provides all the clutter control a laundry room needs. After painting the cabinet, add a tension rod for hanging clothes. Pegs attached to the cabinet sides expand the storage options.

378 shop for flexibility An off-the-rack lazy Susan keeps everything in sight. With a quick turn, laundry supplies are right at hand. Make a pretty container to hold stain-removal pens by covering a pencil box with a scrap of wallpaper.

379 decorative jars Keep small items tidy by storing them in clear glass containers. Print out labels on the computer and attach them with lengths of decorative ribbon.

380 outside the box Mount a folding ironing board on one end of a cabinet. This handy unit collapses neatly when not in use, and storage for newly pressed clothes is just inches away.

For projects and products, see "Dig In" on page 174.

fresh from the *garden*

381 take a dip Keep bath supplies close at hand with a tub-side table. Made of heavy vinyl, this copper-look birdbath is impervious to moisture so it's safe to splash around!

Though designed to be utilitarian, gardening products are often as pretty as they are hardworking. Bring the beauty indoors with these creative storage solutions.

382 new shoes Your garden shoes aren't just for the garden anymore. Bolted to your office wall, they can hold pens and scissors at the ready. Plus, they look pretty gosh-darn cute.

383 small stuff Create an outside-in theme in your office by using petite terra-cotta rose pots to store pins, clips, and other small supplies.

384 tool time Hang your robe and bath supplies in style from sleek garden tools instead of traditional hooks. To mount them, simply drill a hole through the wooden handle (some tools will have predrilled holes for hanging).

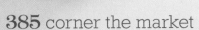

385 corner the market

A corner plant stand can add lots of utility to a small space. Here it contributes convenient—and attractive—storage in a back entry.

386 the cover-up

For out-of-sight storage, add a skirt to the front. This no-sew version is made from two rectangles of fabric, which were hemmed using fusible web and then embellished with self-adhesive trim. Attach the pieces along the front edge with self-adhesive hook-and-loop tape.

387 causing a racket Hung on the wall, a wicker vase holds sports equipment and other items that collect at the back door.

388 child's play Create cool catchalls for toys using sturdy vinyl-coated hanging baskets. Encourage kids' postplay cleanup by mounting them low enough on the wall for little ones to access. No worries about bruises: The thick coating and gentle curves make them kid-safe (just be sure to mount them into wall studs so they can't easily be pulled down).

389 fun and games Traditionally used to carry flowers in the garden, shallow wooden trugs add character-rich storage most anywhere. Find one new online or used at a flea market and use it to store video or board games. When you're ready to play, just carry the container wherever it's needed.

Bring the outside in with **gardenesque storage solutions** that are both fun and affordable.

390

391

390 in the bag With their sturdy canvas construction and plentiful pouches, garden totes are perfect for hauling everything you need for a day at the beach or a picnic in the park. Available in a variety of sizes and colors—you can even get them monogrammed— they're further customizable with decorative ribbons attached with fabric glue. Add a button closure to larger pockets to keep items from falling out. Choose one with trim in a color that coordinates with room furnishings as we've done here, and it serves as a room accessory when you're not on the go.

391 drop in the bucket Hardworking out in the garden, this painted galvanized metal pail also works as the perfect tool in the kitchen to store pasta. To make the divider, cut a piece of white foam-core board to the diameter of the bucket. Cut a second piece to half the size of the first. Bend the larger piece in half and use epoxy to glue one long edge of the smaller piece into the bend of the larger one. Once the epoxy sets, carefully push the insert into the container.

392 climb the wall

A decorative trellis is pretty and practical when mounted on an inside wall. Outfitted with cup hooks, knobs, and wire baskets, this wooden version provides plenty of storage space for kitchen necessities and takes up much less space than expensive cabinetry.

For projects and products, see "Dig In" on page 174.

beyond
bed and bath

Rescued from an ordinary existence in the master suite, these everyday items from the home store now double as storage throughout the house.

393 spick-and-span canisters Glass canisters provide dainty storage for hobby supplies, kitchen clutter, jewelry, and sewing notions. They also organize (yet still display) small collectibles such as matchbooks, marbles, and pins.

394 clever containers
As a decorative alternative to a standard catchall, use toothbrush holders to artfully store paintbrushes, pens, and pencils, and let a soap dish handle business cards and other small items.

395 shoe box storage
Quilters can organize fat quarters by color using these clear boxes. Instead of rummaging through messy bins, they'll find fabrics quickly.

396 in the shower
Create gift central by storing stationery and wrapping paper in a wall-mounted shower caddy. Add ribbon to a wire canister to hang writing utensils from one of the hooks.

397 underbed boxes
Don't have a dedicated crafts room? No problem. Plastic storage boxes keep supplies organized in any temporary work space and are easy to hide under the bed, sofa, or entertainment center.

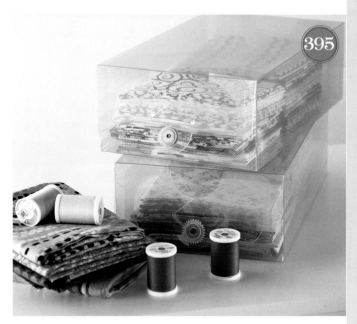

398 smart style Avoid hanger-induced shoulder bumps by draping sweaters over a towel stand, using the extra space below for shoes. The rack fits under hanging clothes perfectly.

399 a little caddy Think of this setup as a portable room of one's own. Stash a journal, reading glasses, and CDs for a movable feast of relaxation. It works nicely for DVDs and remotes, too.

400
pillowcase protectors

Keep occasional-use soft goods (throws, seasonal bedding, and formal dresses) safe and clean with these simple covers that slip over hangers. Slit the seamed end of pretty pillowcases, apply liquid stitching adhesive, and cover the opening with matching bias tape.

401 spruce up spools

A hand-towel bar is just the right size for spools of crafting ribbon. Unscrew the caps on the sides of the bars to add ribbon spools; the caps will prevent the spools from sliding off. You can use the base of the stand to hold coiled lengths.

For projects and products, see "Dig In" on page 174.

shop the $1 STORE

The price is right with these dollar-store finds turned clutter-busting organizers.

402 take a memo An aluminum cookie pan—sans the dough—makes an excellent backing for ephemera and messages posted with decorative magnets. Line the pan with paper and make magnets out of flat-bottom florist's stones. Back the stones with colorful pictures and glue magnets to the back.

405 bank on it Cheap storage containers were meant for food, but they also make great spots for depositing loose change. Assign a denomination to each container and stamp it onto the side. Then cut a slit in each lid and line the containers with fun papers.

403 clean team Enliven a set of plain terra-cotta flowerpots with a coat of hot pink paint and swirl rub-on accents (found with the scrapbooking supplies). These little containers are ideal for storing small bath accessories.

404 cutter-clutter buster No more rooting through drawers looking for just the right cookie cutter. A tabletop-style paper-towel holder provides a slick way to keep them organized. Simply slide the cutters over the dowel, stacking them on top of one another. You'll appreciate being able to easily spot your favorites among the collection.

406 the write stuff Turn a napkin into a tidy solution for organizing a set of colored pencils. Turn to *page 181* for simple step-by-step directions.

407 measured success A hodgepodge of buttons gets organized in style with a set of measuring cups from the kitchen-accessories section. Sort the buttons by color and keep them near the sewing machine so you'll have them at the ready for your next project.

408 on a roll Straw dispensers rise to the occasion to hold towers of ribbon spools. Remove the top of the dispenser inserts and slide the ribbons onto the rods. Not only are unruly ribbons kept in check, but they make pretty displays as well.

409 divide and conquer Intended as a silverware organizer, this drawer insert becomes an efficient spot for storing an assortment of candles. Fit tapers, votives, and a matchbox into the slots and you'll have everything in one convenient place.

410 in the cards Here's a fresh idea for a leftover mint container. Cover both the outside and inside of the lid with decorative paper and place your business cards inside. Use another embellished container for cards you receive.

Search **dollar stores** for everyday items that you can transform into **sensational** organizational accessories.

411 balancing act Declutter the bathroom counter with this tiered caddy that's made with just two plates and a candleholder. Look for matching lightweight plastic plates in two sizes, and glue the smaller plate to the top of the holder and the larger plate to the bottom.

For projects and products, see "Dig In" on page 174.

salvaged storage

If a vintage find strikes your fancy, take it home. You're sure to find a place for it. Here, a need for storage was the inspiration for our latest haul.

412 bin there? Watch for an old bin that has both shelves and cubbies. It's great for organizing small office supplies as well as folders and papers. Use canning or candy jars in the cubbyholes, and outfit the shelves with shallow boxes or baking pans to hold your bills and letters. Mount the bin on the wall over your desk for a functional work center.

413 brain drain With a dishwasher now a kitchen staple, wire drainers are a bit out of favor. Give them new life as holders for file folders. When looking for vintage wire, think beyond the more pricey French garden baskets and bins. This old service item has character and charm and deserves to be put on display.

414 sweet storage A three-hole sugar mold makes the ideal pen and pencil holder for an antiquer. It won't tip over, and it's deep enough to also store scissors, a hole punch, and other desktop necessities. Positioned at the back of the desk, it takes up little space but keeps everything in reach.

415 open-door policy Architectural salvage with worn finishes is great for decorating. Look for door moldings that are the same size and join them to form a box. Install plywood in the bottom for unique desktop storage.

416 grate idea

Small iron grates, designed to sit about an inch off the floor in older homes, look terrific mounted to the wall. By positioning the open edge at the top, you've got the ideal spot for collecting mail and papers. To paint a grate, clean and sand all surfaces before applying metal primer. Then spray on your favorite color.

417 keys to success

No more searching for keys with this clever way to store them right inside the front door—in a drawer that's not out of sight. Install a large sawtooth picture hanger on the back (use two for a big drawer) and hang the drawer. Screw cup hooks into the drawer bottom.

418 savvy storage

An old bin, likely from a general store, turns a pile of shoes into an organized work of art. Label slots with your family's names or let everyone vie for a position. Protect the piece from wet shoes by coating it with weather-resistant varnish.

pages
128–133 Twice as Nice

Pretty Pincushion

Use scrap fabrics and threads to create a stylish and simple pincushion. Even better: Host a get-together with sewing pals and have guests bring their scraps. Send them home with fun and functional party favors.

upclose

Do it! Didn't find the perfect old shelves to refinish? Consider building them yourself. Making basic shelves, such as those on *page 130*, are as simple as selecting board thickness based on what you want to store on the shelves and then cutting them to length. Then sand and finish the shelves as desired before installing them.

On the Hook

Check out these sites for cute storage hooks.

- **Organizeit.com**
- **vandykes.com/ category/hooks**
- **bellacor.com/hooks.htm**

upclose

In the Details

* The bottom drawer of the armoire is big enough to store pots and pans in the kitchen.

* What a bargain! This wire bin comes *with* the island, so you don't have to hunt around for a basket to fit the lower shelf.

We added a cork panel to the inside of the island door and hung tabbed folders for organizing recipes.

* The armoire has lots of drawer space for bath supplies.

pages

138–143 This & That …

Setting the scene A grid of color makes a style statement even when the shelves are empty. Create this look using paint or decorative paper. If your unit lacks a back, color corresponding blocks on the wall.

Small packages, big ideas!
Try these quick ways to add personality to basic storage gear.

upclose

* Insert a tension rod between cabinet sides for easy storage of anything with a center hole.

* Dress up a glass canister with a stick-on decal. Apply decorative papers to plain cardboard boxes using adhesive spray—and decoupage medium if desired.

* Display favorite collections (shells, marbles, corks, etc.) in open or closed glass containers.

144–145 Triple Play

Unfinished business

Buying raw wood furniture, such as the bookcase on *page 144,* and finishing it yourself is a smart way to save money and personalize a new piece. Here's how to properly paint an unfinished wood item.

* Fill in any nail holes or scratches with wood putty; let dry, then sand smooth.

* Wipe down the whole piece with a tack cloth to remove any sanding dust or grit.

* Apply a coat of high-quality primer. The primer creates a surface eager to "grab" onto the paint and will ensure a smooth top coat. Let dry thoroughly according to the manufacturer's instructions.

* Sand the piece lightly with fine-grit sandpaper to smooth any dried drips. Wipe again with a tack cloth.

* Apply the first coat of paint (use semigloss or gloss for the most durable finish) with a brush, sprayer, or paint pad. Let it dry thoroughly, then sand lightly with fine-grit sandpaper. Wipe with a tack cloth to remove sanding dust.

* Apply a second coat of paint, then let dry at least two days before using the furniture. This will allow the paint to fully cure (harden) into a durable surface.

pages
154–157 Laundry Softeners

Opt for moisture-resistant storage (e.g., solid surfaces such as this lazy Susan, or organizers with sealed lids) in a laundry room.

Laundry Organizers

Here's how to help a laundry room work harder.

1. Hang your clothes on a retractable clothesline. When one of the most stylish types is not in use, it's simply a silver circle on the wall. Or use an accordion clothes drying rack that folds against the wall when not in use.

2. Dry a stack of sweaters on the Hamilton Beach Garment Drying Station. It's the perfect size to sit on top of a dryer. Or go low-tech with a standard drying rack. There are single-shelf options that sit atop a dryer, and hanging models you can suspend from the ceiling.

3. Sort laundry into a two- or three-part canvas laundry catchall.

4. Save space with a half-circle hamper. Its flat back hugs the wall.

pages
158–163
Fresh from the Garden

Hang time Make the most of a room by taking storage up onto the walls. Keep things from toppling down with these tips for hanging just about anything:

- **Hang lightweight items** (less than 40 pounds) with screw-in anchors that grip the drywall. For heavier items (up to 70 pounds), use toggle bolts that expand behind the drywall.

- **Very heavy items** (more than 70 pounds) should be attached directly to wall studs, not just drywall.

- **If you live in an older home with plaster walls,** use a power drill that features a hammer setting. It will prevent cracks and crumbles that can happen with regular nails.

- **Brick walls** require special masonry anchors and a masonry drill bit. Drill into the soft mortar between the bricks rather than into the bricks themselves. Mortar can be patched; bricks have to be replaced.

upclose

pages
164–167 Beyond Bed and Bath

An expert tip...
Declutter your bathroom (and stay safe) by disposing of beauty supplies that are more than a year old.

Tuck a desk-drawer organizer into a vanity drawer to house makeup and keep your countertop clear of clutter.

Reinvent your stuff

Taking everyday storage items from one room to another is an easy way to pump up your design without spending a lot of money. For example, an old wooden ladder used as a magazine rack is both decorative and hardworking. Consider these other simple reuses of items you may already have:

* Turn water-resistant containers, such as plastic totes and pails, into hand-towel and washcloth storage.
* Castoff glass bottles and jars can become inexpensive spots to stash bath crystals, salts, and beads.
* An underused filing cabinet can become great sink-side storage for bathroom essentials.

pages

168–171 Shop the $1 Store

Don't waste those leftover boxes, small plastic packages, and empty tins!

Recycle them into something pretty and practical by covering them with decorative papers. Check out these Web sites for a few of our favorite papers:

- **basicgrey.com**
- **makingmemories.com**
- **fancypantsdesigns.com**
- **kandcompany.com**

Make a Pencil Caddy

1. Fold the bottom one-third of a cloth napkin and align the side edges to create a flap; pin.

2. Insert a 6-inch-long piece of ribbon along each side near the top edge of the folded flap.

3. Topstitch the side edges, securing the ribbon ends in the seams, to create a large pocket.

4. Using a disappearing-ink fabric marking pen, mark evenly spaced lines across the pocket, approximately 2 inches apart.

5. Topstitch along the lines.

6. Insert pencils and roll up the caddy. Fasten the ties to hold it closed.

embellish

fast face-lifts

Turn dated flea market finds into stylish home accents using these simple and inexpensive ideas.

419 boxed lunch Decorate a vintage lunch box and thermos with scrapbook paper and stickers attached with decoupage medium. If any areas will remain bare, first cover the surfaces with a paint designed for metal or plastic.

before

before

420 dressed to impress Save a basic hand-me-down dresser with fresh paint. Remove the hardware. Sand and prime the piece. Take out the top drawers and coat them with blue semigloss paint; cover the rest of the unit in white semigloss paint. Add a monogram using a stencil. When the dresser is completely dry, replace the drawers and swap the wooden knobs for porcelain versions.

421 clear choice Turn a plain piano bench into a showcase side table. Remove the hinges from the bench and cut out the center of the top to accommodate a piece of glass. Screw wood trim pieces to each corner on the underside of the top; this will keep the top secure when replaced on the bench. Sand and then prime and paint the piece; let dry. Fit a custom-cut piece of glass to the top using mirror clips. Place decorative paper inside the bench and add photos or a collection.

422 go for the bold Make a '70s-era wicker chair feel modern with color. Cover the chair with spray primer and then gloss spray paint. If the existing cushion is still in good shape, simply re-cover it. Add a flower detail by weaving ribbon through the wicker.

423 shelve the issue Wooden medicine cabinets can still serve a purpose. Sand and then prime and paint the cabinet with latex semigloss paint. Remove the shelves and cover the back with decorative paper. Paint the shelves. Glue buttons to the front.

For more project details, see "Dig In" on page 214.

patio **pots** and **planters**

More than just another pretty pot,
a container is an important design
element in the garden.

424 plant pedestal When it comes
to making a statement, a container needs size,
vivid color, or a dramatic shape (or all three). It
needn't be tall if you can place it on a pedestal.
Look for a sturdy plant stand in wood or metal
and paint it with an exterior finish. Nestle it in a
prime spot in your landscape and top it with a
pot of flowers and foliage.

425 pretty posies in a row If you're looking for a spectacular display, line up your lilacs. After all, they come in lots more colors than their name implies. Paint an old table or metal cart in a bold shade and top it with lilac blooms in shades of white, pink, purple, and blue.

426 pop of color Look closely and you'll see that these succulents are planted in an old bottle crate. Because they require minimal water, they're ideal for growing in walled containers like this. Unless you live in a desert climate, move the box indoors to a sunny south- or west-facing window over the winter months.

427 natural attraction Annual ruby grass makes a striking tabletop arrangement. With stone tiles for bases, this grouping of four becomes a clean, modern centerpiece. If you prefer stronger color, paint terra-cotta pots with acrylic crafts paint and substitute colorful polished-glass stones for the natural pebbles.

428 pick of the season When bearded irises unfurl their pencil-thin buds, you'll fall in love with the color and bloom size. For a sensational centerpiece, fill a vintage watering can with a variety of shades—purple, lavender, yellow, and orange—and enjoy the striking palette wherever there's a space that needs livening up.

429 garden to go Look for vintage little red wagons at garage sales and flea markets and fill them with your favorite flora. Keep the plants in their pots for drainage, or drill small holes in the wagon beds. Be creative in your display. Lined up front-to-back or in a row side-by-side, the wagons will take on artistic form.

430 boxed beauties Not all garden displays need to be fresh-from-the-garden. Here, a wood box displays an artful arrangement of dried narcissus, roses, peonies, hydrangeas, eucalyptus leaves, and daisies with weeping birch branches.

For more project details, see "Dig In" on page 214.

3 plain lamps in a new light!

Embellish plain vanilla shades and bases with stickers, paper, paint, and thread to make lamps that shine with personality.

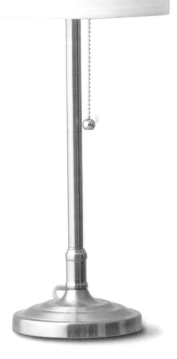

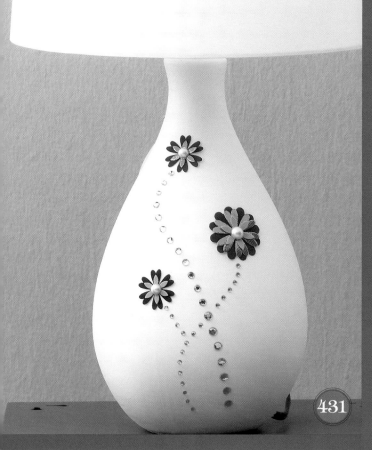

431

432

433

431 petal perfect
When you want a quick yet supercheap face-lift for a lamp base, dimensional stickers will do the trick. Position a trio of flower stickers on the base and add stems using adhesive gems.

432 paper mosaic
Get the look of broken tile without the mess and fuss of traditional mosaic. Cut irregular squares and rectangles from patterned papers, and fit the pieces together on the base using decoupage medium to adhere them. When the base is completely covered, seal the pieces with a coat of decoupage medium.

433 flower power
Make a graphic impact with stylized flowers created with the help of a mask. Made of flexible plastic, the mask is the opposite of a stencil and is easily applied to the base. When you're happy with the position of the mask, spray-paint the entire base. When the paint is dry, pull off the mask to reveal the design.

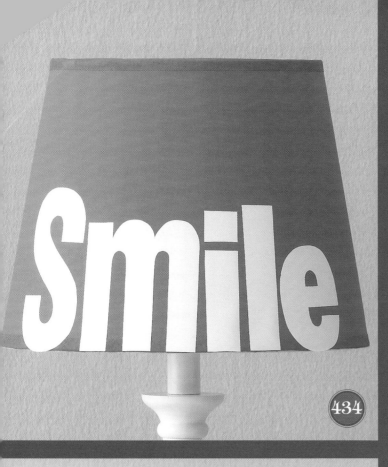

434 word play Greet all who enter a room with a lampshade that's letter-perfect. Decorating the shade couldn't be simpler—just use your computer to print the letters on the back of white adhesive-backed paper, cut out the letters, and adhere them along the bottom edge of the shade.

435 what a stitch Chain-stitched swirls in orange, blue, and lavender add a punch of color to a white lampshade. First use a pencil to lightly draw freehand swirls on the shade; then use an awl to carefully punch holes approximately ¼ inch apart along the lines. Complete the chain stitches using embroidery floss and sewing through the holes.

436 great cover-up Use a large sheet of decorative paper to make a pretty overlay for a plain lampshade. Create a pattern by rolling the shade on the back of the paper and trace along the edges. Cut out the pattern 1 inch outside the lines, and spray-mount it to the shade. Add grosgrain ribbon to the top and bottom edges.

437

438

439

437 ribbon redo Fun zigzag ribbon stripes add a dash of panache to an otherwise bland lampshade. Determine the placement of each zigzag by measuring the circumference of the shade and dividing it by the number of desired motifs. Cut two ribbon lengths for each zigzag and wrap the ends around the shade edges, using hot glue to hold them in place.

438 bloomin' style Paper flowers found in the scrapbooking aisle of a crafts store give this shade garden appeal. Choose an assortment of flowers in a unifying color scheme, poke a hole in the center of each one, and add a pink brad. Hot-glue the arrangement to the sides of the shade.

439 it's a wrap Add personality to a ho-hum lampshade with laser-cut felt ribbon available by the roll. Simply measure the circumference of your shade, cut the felt to length, remove the paper backing, and stick in place.

For more project details, see "Dig In" on page 214.

soft spot

Punch up plain pillows with these easy ideas.
Minimum sewing makes for maximum fun!

440

441

442

440 branching out Pop the seam on the pillow and remove the stuffing for a flat work surface. Using embroidery floss, stitch buttons into a rounded tree shape. Cut a trunk from coordinating fabric and adhere it with iron-on adhesive. Restuff the pillow and repair the seam.

441 boho throw Affix a stencil to the pillow center with low-tack tape. Use more tape to cover areas you don't want painted and protect your work surface with newspaper. Spray on fabric paint and wait a few minutes for the design to partially dry. Remove the stencil. When the paint is completely set (about 24 hours), use the same stencil to add lighter patterns using a stencil brush that's just lightly coated with crafts paint. When all is dry, accent with adhesive gems.

442 nice weave This project is so quick, you don't even need to remove the stuffing to work. Cut lengths of ribbon to fit the front panel of the pillow and attach with iron-on adhesive in a lattice pattern. Don't leave the iron in one spot too long because the heat could melt the batting.

443 great graphic Use a computer to enlarge a letter or clip-art shape to the desired size. Print the image and cut it out. Using the printout as a pattern, cut the shape from fabric and apply to the pillow front using iron-on adhesive.

444 simple slip Cut a length of fabric long enough to go around the pillow, allowing extra length for a seam. Finish the edges by turning them under twice, pressing, and sewing with a simple stitch. Fold the length of fabric in half and stitch closed. Slip the fabric loop over the pillow.

445 to die for Use a die-cutting tool and dies to cut nesting circles of felt. Open a seam on the pillow and remove the stuffing for a flat work surface. Lay out the design and tack the circles in place with pins. Use simple yarn stitches to secure the circles to the pillow front. Restuff the pillow and repair the seam.

446

447

448

446 mock beanstalk Using the pillow's quilted design as a starting point, cut pieces of fabric to fit the shapes. Attach the fabric with iron-on adhesive, then tie a length of ribbon down the center, hiding the knot on the back.

447 leaf motif Outline the existing design with simple running stitches of embroidery floss. Color the shapes using a stencil brush and an ink pad.

448 a need for bead Accent an existing design using seed beads. Instead of sewing on individual beads, string a dozen or so on a length of thread and then stitch them in place. Use larger beads to accent surrounding patterns, looping thread through each one several times to secure it firmly in place.

449

450

451

452

449 ribbon boa Layers of polka-dot grosgrain ribbon create this sassy and easy edging. To make yours, measure the perimeter of your pillow and cut a ribbon to that length plus 2 inches. Place the end of the ribbon length under a sewing machine's presser foot and make a few stitches. As you sew, stitch ribbon loops to the perimeter ribbon. Cut open the loops at an angle, then hand-stitch your trim to the pillow edge.

450 garden style Nostalgia sets in when you lay your head on one of these vintage-look pillows. Crochet a bouquet of fall flowers or gather strips of felted wool to make the blossoms. (Find instructions for dozens of blooms at **crochetpatterncentral .com**.) Cut strips of wool for the stems, and crochet or cut out felt leaves. Arrange and stitch the stems on purchased pillows.

451 modern graphics Try this easy technique for jazzing up a box-shape floor pillow. Cut fabric and fusible material to the same size and shape. Layer the iron-on fusing between the pillow and fabric pieces, cover with a cloth, and fuse with an iron (the manufacturer's instructions for the fusing material will specify whether you should use steam). Test the technique in a hidden spot to ensure the pillow can take the heat.

452 flirty fringe Absolutely irresistible, this is a pillow top you can literally run your fingers through. To make one, hand-sew lengths of mini-tassel trim across the top of any pillow surface (we alternated colors for a variegated look). Start at the bottom and work your way to the top, pressing the tassels down and out of your way as you go. For a round pillow, simply start along the edge and stitch the trim around and toward the center.

453 bleach spots Color on, color off—it's that simple with this technique. Start with a throw pillow with a removable white cover. (Or use white pillowcases or shams from a bed ensemble.) Following the manufacturer's instructions, dye the pillow cover using fabric dye. Choose a stamp with a simple design and apply gel bleach to the back with a foam brush. Stamp where you want to place the design. Let the bleach lighten the color and then wash it out under cold running water.

454 memory pillow For a memo-board pillow, cut lengths of ribbon to fit across the top diagonally in both directions, Secure them in a crisscross pattern with a dab of fabric glue or a few stitches. Sew a button at each intersection.

455 snapshot keepsake To make a photo-transfer pillow, run a color copy of your photo onto a fusible ink-jet fabric sheet. Heat-set the image to printed fabric, trim, and glue it to your pillow. Dress the edges with trims and charms.

456 dream team Cover standard bed pillows with a rich striped velvet and then make an everyday case to go over the top out of washable cotton in a modern floral.

453

454

456

455

FAMI

For more project details, see "Dig In" on page 214.

457

8
ways to dress up windows

Ready-made curtains, blinds, shades, and tablecloths provide the raw materials for these window coverings. We promise they're easy to make—even if all you can sew is a straight line!

460 toss a throw Window treatments don't get any easier than this. Fold over the top of a throw to make a valance. Attach clips to the top edge and hang.

461 pillowcase shade To make a shade from a pillowcase, remove the seams and press flat. Cut the case to size and fuse the hems. Fuse ribbon down the center of the shade.

462 stripe a curtain Horizontal ribbons fused to tab-top curtain panels make it easy to match the colors on the shade.

463 cover up Depending on the size of your window, a shower curtain could be a perfect fit. Stitch a hem at the top and bottom, slide the curtain on tension rods, and cinch the center with a belt.

464 romance with lace Update favorite lace panels by inserting a horizontal band of damask that blocks some of the view.

460

457 add grommets Give a pretty panel a modern touch. Buy grommets in sets of 10 and follow the easy instructions that come packed with them.

458 fuse fabric cutouts Personalize a ready-made shade by selecting a fabric with bold designs that you can cut out. Follow the instructions on the fusible product. Use ribbon along both sides to custom-fit a standard shade to your windows. To let ball fringe show along the shade's bottom edge, remove the cords from the bottom rings on the shade and retie to allow the shade bottom to hang free.

459 add drama Cut coordinating curtain panels in half and stitch them back together with gold trim tucked in the seam between the two colors. It's a clever way to customize curtains to fit your color scheme and a smart way to take advantage of coordinating curtains, since you need only one of each color to make two panels.

For more project details, see "Dig In" on page 214.

chairs with flair

Up a dining chair's style quotient with these easy embellishments, most of which you can complete in an hour or less.

before

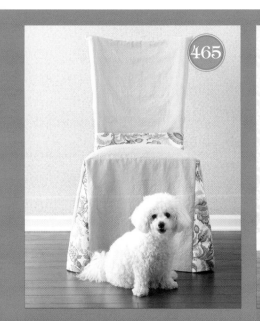

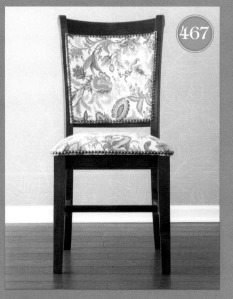

465 under cover Dress up a premade slipcover by adding a fabric sash and panels. For the panels, open the corner seams and sew in a triangle of fabric. Make the sash by sewing two lengths of fabric with right sides facing, leaving an opening for turning. Turn right side out, and then hand-stitch the opening closed. Add hook-and-loop tape to the ends to attach the sash to the chair.

466 puttin' on the glitz For a little shimmer, accent the top edge of a chair with seed beads. Apply a thick layer of decoupage medium and then cover it with beads (the medium will dry clear). Re-cover the seat with a sweater bought at a thrift store.

467 tough as nails Completely transform the look of a slat-back chair by adding fabric panels. Cut poster board to size and then glue on a layer of batting and cover with fabric. Attach the panels using nailhead trim, which is available in a wide range of sizes, finishes, and designs. Cover the seat in the same fabric and finish with more trim around the edges.

before

468 sticky situation If stenciling drives you nuts, use a decal instead. Because the design will be in relief, first paint the area where the decal will go. When it's dry, apply the motif and then paint the entire chair another color. While the paint is still tacky, carefully remove the decal to reveal the design.

469 alphabet soup Make a literary design statement by covering portions of a chair with chipboard letters. Adhere the pieces with crafts glue, and then paint the entire chair. Spray paint is best for this project because it fills the crevices more easily than a brush.

470 heavy metal Add character to a wooden chair by covering parts of it with metal leaf. Spray the area with metal-leaf adhesive before brushing the leaf on. Accent the chair further with a cushion made by sewing together two napkins, right sides facing. Turn and stuff before hand-sewing the opening closed.

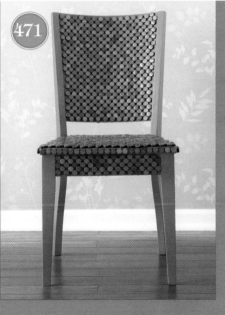

471 full circle Add texture to your chairs with unexpected elements, such as wooden place mats. Choose a smooth-surface design that will be comfortable to sit on. Attach the mats using a strong adhesive, such as E-6000, and cut away the excess with scissors or tile snips.

472 sticker shock Patchwork designs are trendy and easy to create using self-adhesive shelf liner. Cut a trio of papers into rectangles of various sizes (for straight edges, use a paper cutter instead of scissors). Remove the backing and then apply, smoothing out air bubbles as you go.

473 hole in one Lighten a solid-back chair with a little help from your portable drill. Create a template on the computer, tape the design in place on the chair, and then go to work. Save money by choosing a design that utilizes only the drill bits you already own (for example, we used ¼- to 1-inch-diameter circles to match our basic set of bits).

before

clever fixes for
ho-hum
walls

474

Banish boring with two fun and funky paint treatments. Just take a look around your house to find the tools you need.

474 paper-towel circles

After creating a band of color lighter than the wall, stamp rows of circles using a cardboard paper-towel tube.

475 tape rectangles

For a bold backdrop to showcase photography, create vertical bands of color centered on a focal-point wall in your living room. The darker tones in the color blocks allow the white ledge and photo mats to pop.

Creative license: Get a high-end look for less by imitating what you see in a wallpaper book.

beyond the jewelry box...

Necklaces, bracelets, and earrings can get lost in the bottom of a jewelry chest. Keep favorites in plain sight with one (or more) of these clever displays.

476

476 votive holders Add sparkle to glass votives by stacking bracelets on footed candleholders. Vary the colors and styles of the bracelets for an eclectic look. For safety, use only votive candles in glass containers.

477 a little bling Turn a wooden cutlery tray into a beautiful piece of art. Glue scrapbooking papers to the bottom of each compartment using an adhesive that works on paper and wood; secure screw eyes to the cubbies to hold jewelry. Select favorite pieces to fill the tray.

478 bright idea Decorate a paper shade by punching holes evenly around the bottom edge. Clip earrings through the holes.

Find **affordable buys** on vintage jewelry
at thrift stores, flea markets, and yard sales.

479 tieback A vintage pin on a ribbon wraps around a curtain panel for a pretty tieback. Brooches like this one are easy to find.

480 fun frames Jewelry can be art today and an accessory tomorrow. Cover a frame's cardboard insert with decorative paper and suspend a necklace over it.

481 jewelry center Like hat trees, these metal pieces organize and display lots of gear. Use a metal hand-towel stand to hold necklaces and bracelets. Drape pierced earrings and more bracelets from the bars of a decorative metal shelf. Use metal S hooks to maximize how much you can store.

482 runner ready Fringe a table runner by attaching earrings along the edges. Look for a runner made of a fabric that earring wires can easily pierce.

483 knob knockoff Try this project when an earring loses its match. Glue the surviving partner to a flat drawer pull. Make sure the adhesive works on both the knob and the earring material. For matching pulls, use identical earrings.

For more project details, see "Dig In" on page 214.

tricks with trims

Like icing on a cake, trims are the finishing touch on decorating accents. Get a designer look with these tips from the pros.

485

484

484 a shade better Make a stationary window shade using the most amazing fabrics and trims you can find. Sew a lined panel to fit the width of your window and slightly longer than you want it to hang from the inside top. Edge the panel with two trims, layered for interest. Here, soft-blue braided ball fringe is overlapped by chocolate beaded fringe with blue accents in the braid. Mount the top of your shade to thin plywood and install it at the inside top of your window.

485 light show A plain white lampshade is easy to improve upon. All it takes is a yard (or less) of fabric and coordinating trims. We covered this shade in embroidered linen and, along the bottom edge, added elegant glass-bead fringe covered with braided satin cording. Over the top, we hot-glued a distinctive wide ribbon and finished the top with more braided cording.

486 art underfoot Cover any small footstool or ottoman with chenille (a treat to the feet) and give it personality with contrasting trims. We chose blue leopard-print upholstery fabric to go with our potpourri of embellishments, including burlap bullion, high-sheen satin ruched braid with double tassels, and standard upholstery cording with a flange.

487 tame tassels On the ottoman, we pressed cording flange flat and stitched it over the tassel trim to get the look of four trims when we actually used only three.

488 a perfect mat Coordinate your one-of-a-kind accents with a beautiful mirror fashioned from bits of leftover trims. Cover a purchased photo mat with linen, position your trims over the front, and hot-glue the ends to the back. Give an off-the-shelf frame a coat of paint that complements the trims and install a mirror with push points.

489 panel discussion

If your window treatments are looking dated, dress them up with layers of trim. Start 6 to 12 inches down from the top (farther down for pleated panels) and pin loopy-fringe trim across the top. Next, pin wood-bead fringe over the top and add embroidered ribbon so the edge covers the tops of the previous two fringes. Where the panels may have gone unnoticed in the past, now all eyes will go immediately to the texture and colors of the trims.

490 table topper Turn an ordinary table or plant stand into extraordinary art in just a few hours. Purchase a precut circle of plywood from a home center and seal the underside to prevent warping. Cut a circle of fabric slightly larger than the plywood, coat the tabletop with heavy-duty vinyl wallpaper paste, and position the fabric on top, smoothing out any bubbles. Glue the edges over the sides with the paste. (Be careful not to use too much paste and avoid getting it on the top of your fabric.) Decorate the table's edges with fringe.

491 layers of luxury

Trendsetters tell us that velvet and linen are the luxurious "in" fabrics. We used fabric, ribbon, and trim in both these feel-good textures to make a cozy accent pillow. A single pillow with this much texture would surely cost a fortune, but not so when you layer three different trims to get the look.

492 pleated fun

Simple pleated-velvet ribbon decorates the edges of this pillow. The same trim shows up under a wide ribbon down the center.

493 center of attention

Though you may not want to serve up a big pot of spaghetti on a fabulous table runner, it's OK to use one for decorating a table that's not in service. For fall and winter, we made ours from upholstery-grade plaid wool. Because we couldn't find ball fringe that had both the chocolate and teal shades, we used two fringes, one of each color, and overlapped them.

new
cottage
style

Classic floral textiles inspired this space, but our look is light, bright, and thoroughly modern.

494 **stick with it**
Transform any lampshade, photo frame, or mirror in seconds with stick-on dimensional flowers. Edge a shade with a garden of blossoms in summery colors.

494

495

496

497

498

495 arrange for impact
A bouquet of gerbera daisies mimics the bedroom's palette and brings life to the room. Line the vase bottom with colorful buttons.

496 store in style Dress up
any furniture piece with blocks of paint. Shape petals and leaves from nailhead trim; position the trim on the chest until you like the design. Trace the shapes with pencil and paint before hammering the tacks in place.

497 add playful surprises
Scalloped hems flirt with straight legs on our Parsons chairs. Working with a purchased pattern labeled "easy," we first made a test slipcover for the back and seat out of muslin. We saved money by shortening the skirt, which also made for a more playful chair. We spent the money we saved on pretty cording and covered some of the fabric with scraps of curtain eyelet for the pillow.

498 romance a rug Make
a great rug even better and use up your fabric scraps at the same time. Cut scraps into 7-inch-wide strips of various lengths. Press seams open; turn under the edges and topstitch. Depending on the rug thickness and the capabilities of your sewing machine, stitch or glue on the edging. Our 4-inch border features mitered corners.

501 spare the windows A simple shade bedside diffuses direct sun but allows light to fill the room. Bands of narrow ribbon machine-stitched in place create interest without drawing the eye away from the flower-pattern eyelet.

499 mix it up A pile of pillows can
make a small room feel like a master suite. Reserve large floral design for shams or floor pillows. Combining these with stripes, solids, and animal prints updates the look.

500 make it pretty If you own
a sewing machine with embroidery options, let it spin its magic on your bedsheets. If you don't yet own a machine, check fabrics stores or quilt shops for options.

pages
184–185 Fast Face-Lifts

Holes perfected

To make the shelf on *page 185*, you may need to drill a hole that's bigger than the fattest drill bit in your toolbox. So head to the hardware store for a hole saw kit ($20–$30) or a set of wood-boring bits ($15–$20), depending on what size holes you need to cut. Hole saws are meant for holes larger than $1\frac{1}{8}$ inches, while boring bits handle smaller holes.

To create the shelf with glass tumblers, measure the diameters of a tumbler's top rim and its base. The hole's diameter should be right between the two measurements. Outfit your drill with a hole saw attachment of the appropriate size. Mark where the three holes should be, then cut them with the hole saw. Sand any rough edges and remove dust with a tack cloth. Insert the glass tumblers for sparkling storage for small items.

Painting Rattan

Give a beat-up rattan or wicker chair new life with a fresh coat of spray primer and paint. Start by wiping it down with a damp cloth to remove any dirt, and let it dry. Take the chair outside and set it on a sheet or drop cloth to catch any overspray. Shake the can of spray primer according to the label's instructions, then spray 8 to 12 inches from the chair's surface, working in a sweeping motion and overlapping with each pass. Let the first coat dry, then touch up spots you missed or couldn't get to on the first go. Let dry thoroughly. Repeat the same process for the spray paint, again letting it dry thoroughly. Weave contrasting ribbon into flower shapes, securing the ends with glue on the back side, for an added punch of color.

upclose

Vintage luggage labels

During the golden era of travel between the 1900s and 1950s, hotels and airlines across the globe first leveraged luggage labels imprinted with their names, logos, and locations as advertising. Bellhops and baggage handlers eagerly applied these stickers to steamer trunks and suitcases so that wherever a traveler went, everyone could see where she (and her luggage) had been. Today these labels are highly sought after by collectors. Cavallini Papers & Co., a paper company based in San Francisco, made the labels on *page 184*. Vintage-look travel stickers also can be found at **laughingelephant.com**.

pages
186–187 Patio Pots and Planters

In the box

You can turn a wooden pop-bottle crate into a whimsical succulent planter. And it only takes a few minutes. Here's how you do it.

What you need:
- Long-strand sphagnum moss
- Bucket of water
- Wooden pop-bottle crate
- Twelve 3-inch ghost plants
- Twelve 3-inch burro's-tail plants

Make it:

1. A vintage pop-bottle crate from a flea market or garage sale makes a great wall planter. Prepare the sphagnum moss by soaking it in a bucket of water. Squeeze water from a handful of moss; tuck it into the bottom of each crate compartment.

2. Remove one plant at a time from its nursery pot. Wrap each root ball in a handful of wet moss. Stuff each moss-wrapped root mass into a compartment. Tuck in additional wet moss to hold the plants in place.

3. Sprinkle plantings with water. Let the crate sit for a week, allowing the plants time to adjust before hanging the crate. Allow the moss to dry between waterings. To water and feed, take down the planter and let the water drain before hanging it back up.

Happy plants

Container plants can look as good—or as bad—as the care they receive. Follow these steps for beautiful blooms all season long.

✳ **Water.** Nothing drains the life out of potted plants quicker than drought. Water daily, and in the hottest, sunniest locations, consider adding water-saving gels to the soil and catch pans that function as reservoirs.

✳ **Fertilize.** Plants quickly sap nutrients from soil. Replenish with a water-soluble fertilizer every few weeks, or add a slow-release fertilizer to the soil when you plant or repot.

✳ **Deadhead.** Like other garden plants, container varieties need deadheading to encourage continued flowering and a clean appearance.

✳ **Rotate.** Most plants grow toward the sun. Turn containers every few days to keep the growth balanced.

Container advice

✳ **Soften hard edges.** Place containers where they'll disguise harsh edges or angles, either by concealing them directly or by creating a focal point that serves as a distraction.

✳ **Add height.** Gardeners often overlook vertical space. Use freestanding or hanging containers to give your garden new heights of color.

✳ **Unify the landscape.** Use similar or identical containers throughout an area to pull it together. This strategy is especially effective along a path or a long wall or fence.

✳ **Frame entrances.** Doors, gates, and other entry areas are natural focal points. Make a great first impression by framing them with attractive, colorful containers.

pages
188–191 3 Plain Lamps in a New Light

Stitch by stitch

The chain stitch is an embroidery stitch consisting of a series of interlocking loops. Check out the diagram below to learn how to complete the chain stitches used on the lampshade on *page 190.*

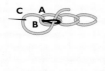

upclose

Word perfect

It's easy to cut letters and words from any printable material. The key is to reverse-print your text so that the letters appear in reverse on the wrong side of your paper. You can flip text in most word-processing programs. After printing the letters, cut out delicate areas first, such as the center of an "e" or "o." Turn the paper rather than your hand or knife for more control as you cut.

pages

192–197 Soft Spot

Pillow talk

Plain pillows can look amazing with the right embellishments. Here's a quick primer on making a basic pillow:

1. Trace two identical shapes on fabric, add ½ inch to each side for a seam allowance, and cut the pieces.

2. Pin the fabric pieces, right sides together (pins should point to the center), then sew. Leave an opening in the middle of one side to insert stuffing or a pillow form.

3. Turn fabric right side out and insert stuffing or form.

4. Turn edges of the opening under slightly and sew closed with a whipstitch.

upclose

upclose

upclose

upclose

pages
198–199
8 Ways to Dress Up Windows

Easy curtain hardware

Clip-on curtain rings are the workhorses of easy-up window treatments. To shorten a curtain without sewing, fold and press the top edge and then clip in place with curtain rings. To minimize the depth of curtain folds, add more rings.

Window Shopping

- Inspect for crooked seams and fabric flaws.
- Check fiber content. Use washable treatments in bathrooms and kitchens.
- Press curtains before cutting apart or adding trims.
- Use washable fabric glue on trims.
- Wash with care, either by hand or in the machine on the gentle cycle.

Grommet kits and fusible web give you no-sew ways to personalize curtains.

Divide to multiply. That's the strategy behind cutting two curtains into sections and creating one new, fabulous window treatment!

204–207 Beyond the Jewelry Box …

1. Try this perfectly simple display idea on for size. Top your dresser with a collection of pretty plates and fill them with your favorite jewelry.

2. Here's a no-fuss way to transform off-the-rack storage items: Line containers, such as this drawer divider, with scrapbooking paper. It's a smart and inexpensive way to add color and pattern. Secure the paper with repositionable adhesive so you can change your palette.

3. Keep favorite pieces of jewelry ready to wear by stringing them from colorful ribbon.

Index